The Unknown Tour de France

The Unknown Tour de France

The Many Faces of the World's Biggest Bicycle Race

Les Woodland

Cycling Resources
books are published by
Van der Plas Publications, San Francisco

Printed in U.S.A.

Published by:
Van der Plas Publications
1282 7th Avenue
San Francisco, CA 94122, U.S.A.
Tel: (415) 665-8214
Fax: (415) 753-8572
vanderp@jps.net
http://www.vanderplas.net

Distributed or represented to the book trade by:
USA: Seven Hills Book Distributors, Cincinnati, OH
Canada: Hushion House Publications, Toronto, ON
Great Britain: Chris Lloyd Sales and Marketing Services, Poole, Dorset
Australia: Tower Books, Frenchs Forest, NSW

Cover design: Kent Lytle, Alameda, CA

Frontispiece: The agony and the ecstasy. Nothing better sums up the spirit of
                  bicycle racing than the statue outside the Madonna del Ghisallo,
                  with the snow-capped mountains of the Italian Lakes behind it.

Publisher's Cataloging in Publication Data:
Woodland, Les
The Unknown Tour de France: The Many Faces of the World's Biggest Bicycle Race.
p. 22.6 cm. Includes index.
ISBN 1-892495-26-0 (paperback original)
1. Bicycle Racing. 2. France. I Authorship. II Title.
Library of Congress Control Number 00-131375

About the Author

ON MANY DAYS, Les Woodland feels as old and rickety as this 1903 Tour de France bike. He has spent 30 years writing about cycling, something his mother insisted was no job for a grown man.

These days, he writes mainly for English publications, but his work also appears in the U.S. In the early days of the U.S. cycle racing bi-weekly *Velo-News*, he was a regular contributor to that publication.

He lives near Norwich in England and Toulouse in France, where Englishmen who know about cycling are as rare as Frenchmen who understand cricket. The thinning hair is due to worry.

Table of Contents

1
The Forgotten Hero

THE GAP between Lens and Sallaumines in northern France is a solemn one. This is world-war country and the battlefield of Vimy Ridge is just to the north-east. Almost 12,000 died there in April 1917 as Canadian troops fought to take the otherwise unremarkable ridge of Nôtre Dame de Lorette.

Thousands of Germans were among the dead and some lie now between Lens and the neighboring area of Sallaumines. The border between the two is the Cimitière Est, off the rue Constant Darras through white stone-pillared gates. The eastern corner is the German war cemetery and few people come. Turn left, though, and walk through the stone chambers, winged angels, and other absurd monuments that constitute a French cemetery, and you come to section F3. A white marker stands ankle-high in the grass. And there, sharing a plot with other members of his family, lies the first winner of the Tour de France. His name was Maurice Garin and I know of no memorial to him anywhere in France. He doesn't even have a gravestone of his own.

Two men in blue overalls look after the cemetery. One is burly with powerful hands. He moves and talks slowly, surprised that anyone should be interested in the life of a grave-digger. He is Jean-Marie Jasniewicz, the son of a Pole who found a new life in France. The other is smaller, a little under average height, with dark grey hair, and more animated. His hands move up and down as much as his eyebrows. He is Maurice Vernaldé and the two share a small office near the cemetery walls, to the left of the gates.

"Our politicians, they have no culture," Vernaldé grumbled to me. "If Garin had been a soccer star or a wartime hero, we'd have a statue or a plaque. But nobody cares about the winner of the first Tour de France."

Lens is not what you'd call an attractive area. The gentle fields and low fences would be innocent enough, were it not for the conical mountains of mining waste, each many times the size of a house. French highways have brown signs to boast of local attractions; so hard-pushed are they around Lens that they show not chateaux or *pigeonniers* or cathedrals but heaps of man-made waste. When Henri Desgrange, the founder of the Tour de France, wrote of pedaling "roseate and dreaming roads sleeping under the sun, across the calm fields of the Vendée, following the Loire, which flows on still and silent," it's possible he overlooked Lens.

"Not many people come," said Jasniewicz. "Journalists now and again, and quite a few Dutch people for some reason. But maybe only one person a year." He fell into a silence, maybe waiting for me to

Maurice Garin, Vainqueur du Tour de France (winner of the Tour de France), read the caption with this title page of **La Vie au Grand Air**, the leading French sports and outdoor magazine, on 24 July 1903. Note that M. Garin is smoking a cigarette.

speak. When I didn't, he volunteered that he'd spent 15 years adding generations to the neat acres of the Cimitière Est before he realized whom he had as his distinguished if silent neighbor.

"There were people from Italian television," he said. "1993, it was. Ninetieth anniversary of the race, and they came and started taking pictures. I had no idea. Until then it had been just another forgotten grave."

Garin was Italian by birth, French by naturalization. He was only 5 ft. 3 in. — Desgrange called him "a little devil" — but his Latin looks and athletic dash must have made him an attractive proposition because he married three times. He divorced wife number one, Jeanne Julie Charlotte Windriff; number two, Catherine Reine Samuelle Cadou, died, as did number three, Désirée Maillé, on May 17, 1952. Garin died five years later, at 4:10 p.m. on February 19, 1957, a month short of 86. He'd lived in Lens for 55 years. A two-column memoriam in the daily sports paper *L'Équipe* said, "In that era, Garin rode a bike as heavy as lead, which demanded enormous strength, power and will. He rode more on pure strength than suppleness. His almost inexhaustible energy let him win the toughest races."

There are no Garins left in Lens. I was going to look them up in the phone book, maybe meet them, but Vernaldé told me not to bother. The family ended with Maurice. The gravestone is a shade more than man-height. Gold capitals in the central dark plaque measure the last heartbeats of the family line. "Familles Brot-Garin et Darnet" says the curved inscription above it. And then, listed vertically in gold:

DÉSIRÉE MAILLÉ
1890–1952
ÉPOUSE DE [wife of...]
MAURICE GARIN
1871–1957
MME VVE BROT
1863–1957
HENRI DARNET
1905–1970
DENISE DARNET
1904–1987

Two small inscriptions in the shape of open bibles have worn away in the weather.

Jasniewicz said, "Now and again I find flowers here and I don't know who left them. And once a month or so I take a broom to the grave and, out of respect, I sweep round him. But apart from that, he's forgotten, I think." By the double gates that marked the end of Garin's last journey, Maurice Vernaldé regretted that the town council wouldn't even prop up the headstone, which he said was beginning to sag. He turned his palms upwards to indicate despair.

"You know that Garin had a filling station in the rue de Lille?" he asked. I did. I'd chanced to stop there to buy a street map when I arrived in the town, but there was nothing to link it with the man who spent his last years there. Nor did it even look the same. Garin bought it from his prize money after the second Tour de France, before disqualification ended his career. In his day the building was square and ugly. Three columns supported a long canopy that stuck out towards the road. Beneath it were metal barrels of motor fluid and above, in square-cornered capitals with dots above each letter I, a clumsily-painted "MAURICE GARIN." In those days the few motorists in the region would have attracted stares as they passed, a new nobility in big black cars that whipped up dust on the unmade roads.

Now it's just another filling station for traveling salesmen and local housewives, opposite a bar for supporters of Lens soccer club, one of the best in France. The bar is painted in club colors. The place across the road is an island of pumps, with a small office for payment and for buying spare bulbs or fan belts. Two women stood with folded arms, discussing one of their husbands. I waited until they'd finished, then approached apprehensively. But no, they said, few people ask about Garin. I even wrote to Elf, the French oil company that sells its wares there, to ask what plans it had for a plaque, or maybe just a photograph. But there was no reply.

"I used to go to the garage when I was young," Vernaldé said. "Of course, Garin was an old man then, a bit stooped, but he still had that enormous moustache. He never lost interest in cycling and he loved talking about it. But I was just a boy then, and old men, they like to tell the same tale over and over again, don't they? I didn't have the patience."

The tale that Garin so repeatedly told is one the history books don't supply. Vernaldé's friendship with the old man with the big moustache explodes one of the longest-lived legends of cycling. But it concerns not the first Tour but its successor, the race that threatened to be the last Tour of all — and all due to the cheating of the little man who lies now in that forgotten grave.

The story about Garin is not so much that he won that first Tour by two hours and 49 minutes, more than two and a half days ahead of the *lanterne rouge* or last man, but that he and the rest of the leaders were disqualified from the second. Legend says three things. The first is that French officialdom still has the two filing cabinets of complaints about that year's race under lock. The second says that among those complaints are that Garin and others expanded the concept of cycle racing by taking a train. And the third insists Garin denied the allegation until the day he died.

I don't know about the secret file. There are stories that it disappeared over the years. But I do know what Vernaldé said about the

Italian television first told grave digger Jean-Marie Jasniewicz that his cemetery included the first winner of the Tour de France. There are no Garins left in town, so Jasniewicz takes it on himself to tidy the grave. You can find it in section F3 of the cemetery between Lens and Sallaumines in northern France. Stand there long enough and M. Jasniewicz is sure to join you.

cheating and the so-called denial: "He admitted it. He was amused about it, certainly not embarrassed, not after all those years. There wasn't the same significance to the Tour then, of course, and he used to laugh and say, 'Well, I was young, *quoi...*' and admit it. Maybe at the time he said he didn't, but when he got older and it no longer mattered so much..."

Garin, with this not inconsiderable help, won the Tour de France again. And then, on November 30, 1904, the Union Vélocipédique de France announced with some understatement that there had been a *violation des réglements*. It disciplined 29 riders. Several — Garin, Lucien Pothier, César Garin and the improbably named Hippolyte Aucouturier — were disqualified. Garin was banned for two years, Pothier for life. The winner, instead, would be Henri Cornet, just 20 years old. The French took to calling him "Le Rigolo" — the fake, or the joker. He's still the Tour's youngest winner. He never again finished in the Tour's top 10, although he did finish third in both the Bordeaux–Paris and the Paris–Roubaix of 1905.

But why wait four months? The answer is that the enthusiasm with which France greeted its new race turned these men into heroes. The UVF's official, Léon Breton, needed time before he dared revive the sometimes dangerous emotions that had made July 2–24 quite so eventful. The French journalist Michel Nicolini recalled, "If they'd taken the decision [to disqualify Garin] at the finish, there'd have been a riot, and lynchings in the ranks of the officials."

Of the six days of actual racing, the Tour's own digest, *Panorame d'un Siècle*, cites "Protests and barricades on the course. Aggression against riders and officials on the col de la République and at Nîmes. Multiple irregularities..."

Spectators organized hit-gangs. Garin and Pothier broke away into the Lyon suburbs only to be cut off by a car full of rival fans. For four miles the driver tried to force them into a ditch. A hundred more fans came out of the morning darkness on the col de la République, let their favorite, Antoine Faure, pass and then set about the rest with staves and stones. Garin wore a white jersey and a sort of yachtsman's cap. He stood out.

"A bas Garin! Vive Faure! Tuez-les!" the thugs shouted. "Down with Garin... up with Faure... kill them!" Pothier struggled past, but neither Garin nor the Italian, Giovanni Gerbi, was so lucky. A bottle crashed on to Garin and Gerbi was clubbed to the ground and

"beaten like plaster," breaking a finger. It would have been a good deal worse if officials hadn't turned up and begun firing shots into the air. Next day, the mobs waited to attack the officials. By now the police had grown alarmed. As the goons grew uglier on the col d'Arles, they pulled their pistols and charged.

When the race disqualified Ferdinand Payan, a rider from southern France, supporters warned that the Tour would "never make it through Nîmes", close to Payan's home town. They threw nails and broken glass on the road. And in the center of Nîmes, they attacked. Again, only gunfire stopped them.

"If I haven't already been killed before Paris, I'll win the Tour again," Garin said on the eve of the stage from Toulouse to Bordeaux. It was gallows humor.

Desgrange fumed. He had the advertising stunt of a lifetime and here it was, falling to pieces. Daily he was getting stories of trees felled, tacks strewn, supporters pacing or even carrying their favorites by car. Word spread of a rider gripping a cork between his teeth, the cork linked to the car in front by a thin steel wire.

Much changed now, but this is the filling station — or its site, anyway — that Garin operated after disqualification from the Tour de France brought his career to an end. There's no memorial to him here or anywhere else in town. You'll find it in the town center.

"The Tour de France is over," he wailed. "Its second edition, I very much fear, will have been the last. It will have died of its success, the blind passions that it has released, the injuries and foul suspicions brought upon it by the ignorant and wicked."

Le Tour de France est terminé et sa seconde édition aura, je le crois bien, été la dernière. Il sera mort de son succès, des passions aveugles qu'il aura déchaînées, des injures et des sales soupçons qu"il nous aura valus des ignorants et des mèchants.

It went ahead, of course. So did the trouble. There were even more sharp tacks next year and the whole race — save a single rider called Jean-Baptiste Dortignacq — wrecked tires on the opening day. But the Tour had been saved and, because Desgrange had turned his wrath on the French authorities for daring to criticize his Tour without providing evidence and for adding punishments beyond those he'd already imposed, he'd also established both himself and the Tour as beyond reproach. Both would grow independent of cycling official-dom, bigger and certainly more arrogant. The power helped the Tour grow but its occasional inability to face criticism hasn't always been to its or to cycling's advantage.

So why has Maurice Garin been forgotten? Why does his home town turn its back? It could be the cheating, of course, but I doubt it. Garin, after all, did genuinely win that first Tour. Perhaps it's just time. Perhaps it all happened such a long time ago. There must be soccer and golfing heroes every bit as important, every bit as old. And every bit as ignored. The Tour de France, I suspect, is simply an everyday fact in France. Utterly splendid but as glorious and as inevitable as sunshine in August.

Garin? Yes, an interesting tale. But to the French, perhaps, no more than any other sportsman from before the First World War.

The First (Very Curious) Race

L INE 2 of the Paris Métro runs into the northern *arrondissements*. The last two stations are Victor Hugo and Porte Dauphine, and the final few hundred meters are beneath the avenue Bugeaud. There, on the surface, is where it all began. It wasn't the Tour de France but it set off the spat that got the Tour started. And it confirmed from the beginning that cycling would sell its soul to the devil.

Bike racing began, not as a recreation for gentlemen, but as a way to sell newspapers. It's been selling everything ever since. Superb riders are covered in banal names, of supermarkets and makers of bottled pop, kitchen fittings and coffee machines. Lotteries use them to sell tickets. They carry the telephone numbers of loan companies. They have been treated so cheaply that one company in the 1970s didn't even correct the misspelling of its own name, printing it one way on shorts and another on shirts. To remember that is to realize why, just as you think cycling might settle for respectability, some fresh scandal will show it hasn't yet lost its touch for the tasteless.

Number 12 in the avenue Bugeaud was the address of the Olivier brothers, who distributed Michaux bicycles through their Compagnie Parisienne. And on Sunday November 7, 1869, they opened before breakfast to prepare for Paris–Rouen, the world's first long-distance bike race. There'd been other races that summer — 34 km from Toulouse to Caraman, for instance — but this would be a whopper, the first real pole-squatter. The longer the race, the more gruesome the demands but also, of course, the more villages in which to sell news. Grimacing, dusty men riding black bicycles faster than anyone could imagine would catch your attention. You'd hear from the paper they were coming, you'd buy another to see who'd won. That's why to this day the world's top races still go from town to town, identifiable but improbable challenges. Think of them: Milan to San Remo, Paris to Roubaix, Ghent to Wevelgem. The Tour of Flanders is run by a paper, so is Omloop Het Volk (which Belgian newspapers other than *Het Volk* call Ghent–Ghent). Milan-San Remo, the Tour de France and Liège–Bastogne–Liège are all linked to newspapers.

"How do you know whether your races sell any papers?" I asked Anton van Melkebeek, a bearded and bespectacled man who was for many years the *grote piet*, the big cheese, of both Omloop Het Volk and the paper itself.

"We don't," he said. "But that's not our main aim. Nor is making a profit from the race, because you can't. Running a race is just spending money, not making a profit. When the race started, years ago, selling newspapers was obviously the aim. Every paper had to have a big

Picture the scene... It was here, at the offices of the Compagnie Parisienne, that riders gathered to collect their maps and numbers for the great race from Paris to Rouen. Many had been in the city for days and the tension was so great that the ride to the start — they turned left out of that double door — turned into the race itself and half the field didn't stop to line up.

race to its name. Now the race is just a billboard. Ultimately, of course, selling more papers is the aim, but that's not the primary reason the way it was in the past. Now it just keeps our name in the public eye."

Paris—Rouen was run by *Le Vélocipède Illustré*. It's hard to realize, now that Coca-Cola and others make no pretense of their commercial interest, that sponsorship was almost unknown. *Le Vélocipède Illustré* needed more than advertising to justify itself; it needed a cause. It procured 1,000 francs and a bike from the Compagnie Parisienne and announced on September 30: "To further the good cause of the bicycle, it must be determined that the bicycle can be raced over considerable distances with incomparably less fatigue than running. By seeing for itself, the public will be able to appreciate the real merit of the bicycle that makes a maximum economy of time and energy. Therefore we announce to our readers that a first long-distance race will take place in late October. The distance to race will be that separating Paris from Rouen, being a distance of 130 kilometers approximately." The rules said competitors were not "to be trailed by a dog or use sails."

The winner was a slender 19-year-old called James Moore. The French took him for their own because when he was four years old in 1854 his family moved from Bury St Edmunds in eastern England to an alleyway between the avenue Montaigne and the Champs Elysées in Paris. The French called him "Jimmie Meer."

It took him 10 hours and 25 minutes to cover 134 km, not much more than twice walking speed. The distance was so vast, riders so poorly prepared, bicycles so heavy, and above all the roads so bad, that that was as fast as the racers could go. The marvel is not that they went so slowly but that they could go that fast. A letter to the organizers gives an idea of how awful things were:

> I made, on October 7 with some friends, the journey from Paris to Rouen. Leaving at 6 a.m. from Vaugirard, we were forced to stop at 8 p.m. at St.-Clair-sur-Epte, 12 leagues from Rouen, because of the bad state of the paths. We were also suffering from fatigue; it came from being such a long time in the saddle, a pain that made itself felt forcibly.
>
> Leaving Paris at St.-Germain and going through Saint-Cloud, Suresnes, Rueil or through Neuilly, Courbeboie, Nanterre, the roads are fairly good. From Poissy to Triel there are only paths in bad condition. It would be better to go up to the Chanteloup plateau to regain the road from

Pontoise to Magny and Puiseux. Between Meulan and Averne, the road is tarred and very pleasant, but it will be impossible to climb Averne hill by bike because of its deplorable condition.

A Monsieur Deroisier said, "it seems to me you've made an error in obliging competitors to pass through Louviers, unless you have a particular fondness for the place." The road was of terrible cobbles, he said, which he knew "only too well." The race skipped Louviers and went through Pont-de-l'Arche instead.

There were 325 at the start. The idea was to ride to the avenue Bugeaud between 6 and 7 a.m. to collect the paperwork — "all *coureurs* will be given, before the start, a special map of the road from Paris to Rouen, drawn up specially for them and which will give them the necessary information" — and then along the avenue Victor Hugo to the Arc de Triomphe, built only 33 years earlier at the head of the avenue Champs Elysées.

Many riders had been in Paris for several days, relaxing and searching the bike shops along the avenue de Wagram for the latest equipment. They were anxious because of the terrible journey ahead but also because the rules warned them not to be late — "The planned start, place de l'Étoile [Arc de Triomphe] at 8 a.m. precisely, will be given without waiting for latecomers, who will be able to start late and catch the race if they can."

Nobody knows how many there were because so many enthusiasts joined in for fun. Crowds by the roadside began cheering. The first 50 riders grew convinced the race had started and the speed

Crop of gold — James Moore's medals and trophy from his pioneering bike races are in the museum at Ely, north of Cambridge, England.

picked up. The more it rose, the more the crowd applauded and the more sure the riders became that racing had begun. They rocketed down the avenue de Neuilly (now the avenue Charles de Gaulle) and off to Rouen. They left even before the organizer, one of the brothers Olivier, got to the start. He "expressed strong astonishment that they had not waited for him." Stewards had to promise riders left at the start they they'd have 30 minutes deducted from their time in compensation.

Nobody had pneumatic tires. Most rode on plain steel rims. Moore had solid rubber fixed to his rims, and ball bearings made by the city's prisoners, as befitted the winner of the world's first race, 1,200 m from the fountains to the entrance gate of the Parc Saint-Cloud in Paris and back again in March 1868. His bike, with pedals on the front wheel, came from Ernest Michaux, a childhood friend whose 250 workers produced 12 bicycles a day in the rue Jean-Goujon. He and other Michaux riders tossed a coin to decide who was to ride it.

There were other foreigners as well, including a woman who despite British parentage styled herself Miss America. She was cheered wherever she passed. To compete under a false name was a fashion, even a necessity. Cyclists were considered cranky and many didn't fancy the derision. Among the 201 who entered in advance were Pe-

James Moore, a little thickened from his youthful self by a successful life in horse racing, returned to northern London as he grew older. He died there after a prostate operation. Nobody knows where he is buried. The bike, however, is in the museum at Ely.

ter The First and Johnson of Brussels. There were two Johnsons, numbers 67 and 270, one a Londoner called J.T. Johnson, who rode in a jockey's silk shirt, colored cap and jacket, kid breeches and gaiters. He carried a whip "to keep off the dogs." He was second into Bonnières at 12:45 p.m. and then paid for his rapid start. He ground to a halt at Vaudreil after 60 miles. Local cyclists manning the signing-on control ran up to him.

"What's the matter, Johnson?"

"I'm shattered."

"Get off your bike."

"I can't."

They carried him, literally, to the home of Monsieur Duval, the head of the train station, laid him down, undressed him, rubbed his legs and gave him warm wine. Johnson told them he'd ignored the race doctor's advice and eaten just two sandwiches. Duval fed him and left him to sleep. When word spread, a local moneybags insisted on taking Johnson home for dinner. The Londoner, no worse than many a cyclist who has ridden too far and eaten too little, was happy not to refuse. And an hour later, fed, washed and content, he told his host "Well, thanks a lot. I'd better be going." He scampered up the road, passed one competitor after another, regained the hour he'd lost and finished seventh.

The *arrivée* was across the road from St Paul's church in Rouen, outside a café lit by Venetian lamps. Moore, who'd been in the second start from Paris, turned up in darkness at 6:10 p.m. He'd averaged seven miles an hour. Somebody stole his bike. André Castéra and Jean Bobillier —— the latter on a farmer's bike weighing 35 kg — arrived a quarter of an hour later and asked to be considered joint runners-up. Miss America finished at dawn next day and won a prize as the only woman inside the time limit.

Moore won the vast sum of 1,000 francs, a medal, and a cup. He went on to work as a vet, like his father, trained race horses for Maisons Lafitte, is said to have taken up golf with an eight handicap and to have been an excellent runner. He served in the ambulance corps during the siege of Paris in the Franco-Prussian war and died a *Chevalier de la Légion d'Honneur.* Like all the others, though, he had to pay his own fare back to Paris. The organizers helpfully explained it would cost 8 francs 40 centimes.

3
Enter Henri, the Magnificently Crazy

PARIS–ROUEN gave organizers huge ideas. Look at France and see how far Bordeaux is from Paris. It's so distant that the race between the two was paced by tandems, cars, and then by little motorcycles called Dernys, half-pedaled, half-powered. One of the happiest distractions in cycling for years was to see the pompous and overweight Derny-pacers riding in comical crash helmets, their backs upright and toes pointed out for maximum shelter, sponsors' jerseys stretched over spinnaker bellies.

And yet even Bordeaux–Paris wasn't enough. Pierre Giffard, a part-timer at *Le Petit Journal,* said he "wanted a race that went to the end of the earth." And so he ran one, from Paris to Brest and back, his little joke being that Brest is in the province of Finistère — literally, the end of the earth. Those who knew about these things said nobody would ride 800 miles. But they did. Giffard had 600 entries and 206 starters on the morning of September 6, 1891. The French champion, Charles Terront, won after having to find a marshal who'd gone off for a doze, despite breaking his chain and after five times flatting the pneumatics that Edouard Michelin had fitted to his Humber. Many of the flats were from nails fallen from hobnailed boots. And it says why so many cyclists were doubtful about pneumatics when you realize that it took a Michelin mechanic 40 minutes to make one of the repairs.

Terront was second into Brest, stopped for six minutes and then set off again for Paris to win by seven and a half hours. Note that's not in seven and a half hours… it's *by* seven and a half hours. Ten thousand cheered him back to the Porte Maillot on the edge of central Paris.

Desgrange reported these races with a style verging on histrionic. "There are four of them," he wrote. "Their legs, like giant levers, will power onwards for sixty hours; their muscles will grind up the kilometers; their broad chests will heave with the effort of the struggle; their hands will clench on to their handlebars; with their eyes they will observe each other ferociously; their backs will bend forward in unison for barbaric breakaways; their stomachs will fight against hunger, their brains against sleep. And at night a peasant waiting for them by a deserted road will see four demons passing by, and the noise of their desperate panting will freeze his heart and fill it with terror." It was an enviable style, creating expectation without a single fact.

Desgrange was himself no mean cyclist. He set the world's first hour record, at Neuilly, Paris, in 1893. Thirty-five kilometers, or 22 miles, is nothing today but it was impressive at the time. Photographs show a long-faced man, stern in the style of the day — he was born in 1865 — but word says he was lively, flamboyant enough to be fired as a legal clerk after a woman client saw him cycling with bare calves. But he was cautious, too, investing in a chain of cycle tracks that gave him connections in the bike industry. He resented the power of men like Pierre Giffard, who not only freelanced for *Le Petit Journal* but also edited the sports daily *Le Vélo* in the rue Meyerbeer in Paris. Desgrange

He looks odd, even slightly wet in his sandals. But Henri Desgrange held the world's first ratified hour record and showed the same hardness in the way he treated not only riders in the Tour de France but the whole of cycling officialdom. Within a few years he had made himself bigger than the whole of organized cycling and, within a couple of decades, his race had become the whole purpose of professional road racing.

was running the publicity service for Adolphe Clément's tire factory, which meant keeping in with Giffard, and if he was wondering what to do next then Giffard unknowingly gave him his opportunity.

It had nothing to do with cycling, everything with French passion. Giffard took sides in the case of Alfred Dreyfus, an army captain from Mulhouse near the Swiss border convicted in 1894 of passing secrets to the Germans from his job at the war ministry and exiled to Devil's Island in French Guiana. Dreyfus was Jewish and France split over whether an anti-Semitic officer called Major Esterhazy had forged the evidence. *Le Vélo* claimed Dreyfus was guilty, but when Giffard wrote for *Le Petit Journal* he insisted Dreyfus was innocent and that Esterhazy should be guillotined. More, he stood up at an anti-Dreyfus demonstration on the horse-racing course at Auteuil and said so.

Unfortunately, among the *anti-dreyfusards* there that day was the Comte de Dion. For some reason the police arrested him. Giffard knew Dion as the founder of the Automobile Club de France and visited him in jail There they argued violently, leading Giffard to write his editorial backing Dreyfus. He was both brave and foolhardy. Dion stumped up much of the money behind the paper and he wasn't a man to be told he was wrong. He pulled out his money and took other advertisers with him. It was a hefty blow. There were a dozen sports papers in France and they were all scrapping for advertising.

Let us discuss this over lunch, Henri Desgrange told Géo Lefèvre. The words "Tour de France" had just been spoken for the first time in **L'Auto**'s offices on the middle floors of this office block in the rue Faubourg Montmartre. The two men emerged from the doorway beneath the Video Club sign and turned left up the gentle rise towards Desgrange's favorite restaurant.

Giffard was now De Dion's enemy. And if Giffard had *Le Vélo*, then De Dion would strike back. He turned to Clément, to Michelin, and to other *anti-dreyfusards,* such as the Baron Zuylen and the Comte de Chasseloup-Laubat, and together they set up a new paper. They knew of Desgrange because he'd written for *La Bicyclette,* for *Paris Vélo,* and for other rivals to *Le Vélo.* He'd written a training manual called *La Tête et Les Jambes* and every morning he rose for physical exercises and a fast walk, a habit he kept for the rest of his life. He was an obvious editor.

It's interesting to reflect that Desgrange gained his paper thanks to the persecution of a Jew — Dreyfus was eventually pardoned in 1906 — and that it was closed not long after his death for continuing to publish under the Nazis. It's dangerous to use the present to judge the past but another glimpse of Desgrange's attitudes is revealed in his treatment of the first black world champion, Major Taylor.

Desgrange attracted 30,000 to his Parc des Princes track on the edge of Paris to see the American sprint against Edmund Jacquelin, the champion of the day. The prize was $7,500, worth a dozen times as much today. The historian Peter Nye says that when Taylor beat the favorite in two straight rides, "his triumph was so upsetting to race director Henri Desgrange (...) that Desgrange paid Taylor in 10-centime pieces — coins like dimes — and Taylor needed a wheelbarrow to carry his winnings away."

Victor Goddet, the manager of the Vélodrome de l'Est, became financial director, and he and Desgrange set up *L'Auto-Vélo.* They picked yellow paper because Giffard used green. Their creation first appeared on October 16, 1900, in the closing days of the World's Exhibition and the Olympic Games in Paris.

Desgrange then made another inspired choice. He went to *Le Vélo* and offered a job to Géo Lefèvre, a 26-year-old as keen on rugby as cycling, who'd thrown in his studies to be a reporter. Lefèvre was dutiful and told Giffard that Desgrange had approached him but that he hadn't yet taken the job. Giffard flew into a not unusual temper and fired him. Lefèvre went straight to Desgrange and took his offer.

Including *vélo* in *L'Auto-Vélo* was too close for comfort for Giffard. He complained the title was too like his own — almost certainly Desgrange's intention — and on January 15, 1903, a court agreed. Desgrange shortened it to *L'Auto* and then for fear that customers would think it was interested only in cars, he added "Motoring, Cycling, Athletics, Yachting, Aero-navigation, Skating, Weightlifting, Horse Racing, Alpinism." It didn't do much good. Giffard sold three times as many papers.

Time and again Desgrange failed to come up with original ideas. *Véloce-Sport* organized Bordeaux–Paris, and Desgrange ran another one three months later. Readers stayed away and the bosses grew anxious. And it was then that Desgrange could bless the day he took on Lefèvre. On the morning of November 2, 1902, the two were at the long table on the first floor of 10 rue du Faubourg Montmartre in Paris, between the Gare St. Lazaire and the Gare de l'Est train stations and just round the corner from the old Folies-Bergères. The street was to stay headquarters of the Tour until they moved to the suburb of Issy-les-Moulineaux 90 years later. Downstairs, where Goddet held sway, and above him on the editorial floor, the atmosphere was despair. Circulation was stuck at 20,000, the owners were losing money, and Giffard seemed unshakeable.

"What we need is something to nail his beak shut," Desgrange famously said. He looked at Georges Prade, the third man present and then at Lefèvre, who paused and then answered: "Let's organize a race that lasts several days, longer than anything else. Like the six-days on the track but on the road. The big towns will welcome the riders." Legend says there was a silence. Desgrange, unconvinced, eventually said, "If I understand you right, *petit Géo*, you're proposing

It was here, in this restaurant, that Desgrange waited until coffee before asking Lefèvre to explain this Tour de France idea again. Desgrange, typically with new ideas, wasn't sure and said he'd ask the firm s financial boss. To his surprise, Victor Goddet agreed, and the Tour de France was born soon after Desgrange and Lefèvre put away their napkins and returned to the office. The restaurant has much changed since Desgrange's day. It's a youthful beer-and-music set-up these days, but the management knows its history — an alcove has been set aside to commemorate the day France acquired the world's greatest race. The commemoration is at the back of the bar to the right.

a Tour de France?" The word *tour* in French is more akin to the English "circuit" than to leisurely exploration.

"And why not, *patron?*" said Lefèvre.

Desgrange was dubious. He hesitated, looked at his watch, announced it lunch time and led Lefèvre to the Taverne Zimmer in the boulevard Montmartre. The subject wasn't mentioned until coffee and then Lefèvre ran through it again. Desgrange said no more than that it was "interesting" and that he'd mention it to Goddet, who held the money. Goddet would pooh-pooh the idea, saving further decision. But to Desgrange's surprise he agreed. And in a single column on January 19, 1903, *L'Auto ("Automobile, Cyclisme, Athlétisme, Yachting, etc")* announced the greatest bike race in the world.

MAURICE GARIN
Vainqueur de la course Paris-Brest

Maurice Garin was France's great star and won the monstrous Paris–Brest–Paris. But he wasn't born French. His birthplace was Italy and he joined his father in his emigration north and soon took French nationality. You may notice a decline in the dress standards of race officials since 1901...

Everybody got the glory, except Lefèvre, who after 1904 was steered towards other sports. Desgrange usurped the title of Father of the Tour. Even the café shared the fame. The Taverne Zimmer turned into the Madrid and then into TGI Friday's, and a plaque on the wall now celebrates *"la plus grande compétition sportive du monde."* It certainly was. *L'Auto* said it would leave Paris on June 1, 1903, and go to Lyon, Marseille, Bordeaux, and Nantes before finishing in Paris on July 5. To this extent, as Georges Conchon said in a remark much favored by the organizers, "The Tour [did] more for the national unity of France than any of the major events the country has witnessed in the 20th century."

Pierre Giffard wanted a race to the end of the world and back. It was his play on words and geography. There's probably some reason why the bunch is split in two but the caption doesn't explain. The building in the background is Giffard's editorial office, forced to close after competition from the Tour de France. The modern P–B–P, no longer a race but still ridden by some as though it was, is in the western suburb of St.-Quentin, rather less glorious.

It was a time for big ideas, big gestures. The Wright brothers flew their first airplane, Henry Ford was opening factories, William Harley and Arthur Davidson decided to make motorcycles, and America made its first cowboy film. Other newspapers enthused about the idea. Giffard ignored it. Lefèvre sneered on January 19, 1903, that "the newspaper that calls itself *Le Vélo* doesn't deign to give a line — not a single line, mark you — to the this most sensational *vélo* race organized since the invention of the bicycle. So are the readers treated." Giffard's bluff was called. Next day he gave precisely 11 words to the race, without once mentioning Desgrange's newspaper.

Of more concern was that the riders weren't interested either. They went far enough in Paris–Brest–Paris, and more than a month from home did nothing for them. Desgrange backed down. He cut the race to three weeks, halved the entry fee to 10 francs, and offered five francs a day to the first 50. He added Toulouse, to save crossing all southern France from Marseille to Bordeaux in one day, and raised the prizes to 20,000 francs. Still it didn't work. By June 5 he was pleading. Riders would spend no more than if they stayed at home, he said. Hoteliers would give them cheap meals for the honor of having them stay. You could sense the implied "Please, *please*, ride my race."

I once had the privilege of talking to Pierre Chany, the first journalist to follow 50 Tours and one of the greatest — and often most imperious and once most hard-drinking — reporters of cycling there has ever been. He'd been contemptuous that no Frenchman had made the winning break at a world championship in south-east Holland and turned his back on the TV in the press room and pointedly read a paper instead. He told me, "Desgrange always believed in the Tour from the moment he shortened it and the riders became interested. But he wasn't so sure that he wanted to stake his personal reputation by following it himself. He didn't visit the race until it had been going for several days."

Lefèvre described his boss as "a hard man, in the good sense of the word." It was a generous gesture, given that Desgrange told him to follow the race by bike and by train as organizer, referee, judge, timekeeper, and statistician. And in the evening, there being an ounce of energy still remaining, he and his colleague Olivier Margot could write a full-page account of the day.

The First Tour

THE MONEY that Victor Goddet put into that first Tour was not to be sneezed at, even if you had a moustache as large as George Abran's. Abran was the starter that unusually warm first day of July 1903 and he turned up outside the Café Réveil Matin in a general's uniform, his white moustache glorious above the accompanying beard.

Goddet was offering 3,000 francs for the winner, 2,000 for the runner-up, and 1,000 for the daily winners. Each day awarded:

Stage 1: Paris–Lyon (476 km):
> 1,500, 700, 350, 200, 100, 100, 50, 50 francs.

Stage 2: Lyon–Marseille (374 km):
> 1,000, 450, 250, 125, 75, 75, 50, 50 francs.

Stage 3: Marseille–Toulouse (423 km):
> 800, 350, 200, 100, 75, 50, 50, 50 francs.

Stage 4: Toulouse–Bordeaux (268 km):
> 700, 300, 200, 100, 75, 50, 50, 50 francs.

Stage 5: Bordeaux–Nantes (394 km):
> 1,200, 500, 250, 125, 100, 75, 75, 75 francs.

Stage 6: Nantes–Paris (471 km):
> 3,000, 2.000, 1.200, 800, 500, 250, 200, 100, 50, 50, 50, 50, 50, 15 francs.

A workman earned just 25 centimes an hour, or two and a half francs for a 10-hour day. A kg of bread cost 40 centimes, or less than half a franc. So the 6,075 francs that Maurice Garin won in Paris amounted to 2,400 days' pay, or nine years' work without a break — and tax was only 7.5 percent. To put that in perspective, the winner's prize by the mid-1960s was less than three years' pay for a semi-skilled worker, with tax about four times as high.

Comparisons with modern prizes are confusing because France turned each of its francs into only 10 centimes when it switched to "new francs" after the war. But it's true that prizes moved ahead of inflation between the mid-sixties and the start of the 1990s, from about $52,000 in total to more than $1.5 million. In 1998 it was 12 million francs, or approaching $2 M. The figures are difficult to calculate in dollars because of different exchange rates over the years, but that gives an idea.

The adventure begins... with a scruffy hand-drawn map. Desgrange gave his riders nicknames of his own invention and, in the days before newspaper photos, ran hand-drawn sketches of Aucouturier, Fischer, and Garin. Desgrange was proud enough to name himself as editor beside **L'Auto**'s title but not so convinced of his race that he wanted to follow it.

The Café Réveil Matin wasn't such a strange place to start. Remember it was simply *a* Tour de France. It hadn't become *The* Tour de France. Nobody knew there'd be a second, let alone another 90 years' worth.

The mail coach from Lyon used to change horses there before going on to the capital. There were stables with rooms for horsemen. Two were murdered in the hope they were carrying gold and their deaths were turned into a stage play. The bar had a reputation for steak and fries. It welcomed cyclists when cyclists weren't always welcome. Local races started there, so Desgrange knew its name and may even have visited it to report for his paper. Certainly he knew the family that owned it.

It's not easy to find from central Paris even now, although there are enough visitors to justify a sign from the main road. You leave Paris by the Porte Dorée on the *périphérique* ring-road, ride alongside the Bois de Vincennes, where Jan Janssen became the first Dutchman to win the Tour — by 38 seconds, in 1968 — and then on to Route Nationale 19 to Montgeron. Then the village was a mere few souls of whom only a few had seen the Champs Elysées, 19 kilometers away. Now there are 22,000 and I don't suppose they give the Tour a

The Réveil Matin was well known to bike riders in 1903, although then it was deep in the countryside rather than on the city's outskirts. The name means "morning call" or, by extension, "alarm clock." The riders of 1903 would recognize the bar if they returned today. Little has changed beyond the road junction now having a small pedestrian island.

thought unless it blocks their path. The Réveil Matin stands by a T-junction, the meeting of the Melun and Corbeil roads, just as it does in the sepia 1903 photograph on the restaurant menu. A plaque on the side wall announces:

ICI

devant le RÉVEIL MATIN

le 1er JUILLET 1903

fut donné le départ du

1er TOUR DE FRANCE

organisé par HENRI DESGRANGE

Further engravings announce the Tour's 50th visit and another in 1979, the 66th Tour. It's a pricy restaurant these days, with a separate bar. I fell to talking with an old boy who sat in the corner nearest the plaque. He was drinking a *demi* of beer. I never asked his name, nor he mine.

"Must have been quite a day," he said. "It'd have been good to have seen it." He took another sip in the manner of old boys everywhere.

"I don't suppose there's anybody alive now who did?" I asked hopefully, spirits falling as I did the figures in my head.

"Not that'd be worth talking to," he said with a chuckle. "Even babies would be around a hundred now." Silly question.

We walked through the double door and into the road. The Montgeron sign is across the road, the main village to the right. To the left is a refuge in the junction for the road from Paris.

The Réveil Matin still has its bar where the riders gathered. Sadly, all the memorabilia from the turn of the century have gone, stripped from the walls by souvenir robbers. On the side of an external wall is a large plaque marking the pub's reputation and recalling the day the race again visited its birthplace.

A line of trees grows along the opposite pavement. It looks almost exactly as it did in 1903.

"Which way did they set off?" I asked.

My friend shrugged.

"I think that way, *monsieur*," he said, pointing towards the Paris road. "They changed in the cellar and came out of the café and gathered behind barriers in the street, but I've never asked which way they set off." I discovered later that they'd gone off towards Corbeil, a collection of *types* in caps, jackets, and long pants — more or less their working clothes — dressed for endurance rather than speed.

I'd asked if there'd be anybody who recalled it and been shown to be over-ambitious. Still, things move slowly enough in Montgeron to make it possible. Raymond Potteau, who owned the bar when the Tour grew 90 years old in 1993, was himself 79 at the time and had bought it from his in-laws soon after the war. They in turn had had it since the 1920s. His barman, Lucienne Robin, worked there for 60 years. It was Potteau who extended the café and added the restaurant, which gained two stars in the Guide Michelin. You can look into the cellar where the racers changed and you can sleep among their ghosts; the Réveil Matin is also a hotel. The one thing you can't find is a souvenir. They've all been stolen.

You can imagine the tension at *L'Auto*'s offices on the night before the race — the boxes of armbands and red badges, the paperwork, the enthusiasts wearing boaters. Street singers and mandolin players turned up in Montgeron next morning, and salesmen to sell Coco, the Coca-Cola of its day. All that remain are a few photographs and Margot's description of 3:16 p.m. that afternoon: "The men waved their hats, the ladies their umbrellas. One felt they would have liked to touch the steel muscles of the most courageous champions since antiquity. Yes, the most courageous because — a revolution in our splendid sport of cycling — the race will be run without pacemakers except on the final stage. An end to the combines and ruffians of every stamp. Only muscles and energy will win glory and fortune. Who will carry off the first prize, entering the pantheon where only supermen may go? I do not hesitate to make Maurice Garin, the white bulldog, my favorite."

Garin, whose pedigree included winning the Paris–Roubaix of 1897 and 1898 and coming third in 1900, was more usually known as "the chimney sweep," but *L'Auto* gave nicknames to the riders even if they already had one, to familiarize them to readers. 1905 was the most prolific year; Louis Trousselier was called *La Fleuriste* because his family ran a flower shop. René Pottier was *Le Boucher* because of the family butchery.

There was, in fact, another favorite, Hippolyte Aucouturier, a man in a red and blue jersey and built like a wrestler who'd recently won Paris–Roubaix and Bordeaux–Paris. He had the speed but Garin had the endurance, which he'd shown by winning Paris–Brest–Paris earlier in the year. Aucouturier, though, had frequent stomach problems. Critics said he drank too much water.

The German champion, Josef Fischer, was also there, a specialist in what we'd now call "ultra" races. And an odd collection of others. There was Jean Dargassies, a blacksmith from Grisolles, near Toulouse; his first bike ride had been only two months earlier and he'd never heard of the Tour until his bike shop told him he looked strong enough to ride. There was a tourist called Jean Desvages, who wanted little more than to see a bit of France but nevertheless came 20th. He rode every year to 1910 but never again finished. Others now long forgotten became the "champion of the carpenters," the "heel pedaller," the "prince of miners."

Of the 76 who started only 21 finished. The field was made up of 60 professionals and a smattering of *partiels*, who'd entered selected stages. Among them were 13 amateurs who wanted to ride from Toulouse to Bordeaux. Eventually Desgrange had to set the professionals off an hour before the *partiels* to stop the fresher dilettantes helping the real Tour men. On the morning of the start, he used the width of the front page to proclaim:

LE TOUR DE FRANCE — LE DÉPART
Organisé par L'AUTO du 1er au 19 Juillet 1903

A four-column map dominated the page and, under the heading "The seed," he excelled himself: "With the broad and powerful swing of the hand which Zola in *The Earth* gave to his ploughman, *L'Auto*, newspaper of ideas and action, is going to fling across France today those reckless and uncouth sowers of energy who are the great professional riders of the road." It was then that he began waxing about racing "madly, unflaggingly... from Marseille to Bordeaux, passing along the roseate and dreaming roads sleeping under the sun, across the calm fields of the Vendée, following the Loire which flows on still and silent." It was easy to write like that. The reality for Lefèvre was different.

"For the final time, the pack has forced itself in the night," writes Géo Lefèvre, "the controls lit up and blinding, and soon the giants of the road will reach the goal that lay 2,500 km ahead of them when they first climbed into the saddle." To which Desgrange added: "I have had many sporting dreams in my life but I never dreamed of anything like this." Not a single front page but an amalgam from the week of June 28–July 3, 1903.

35

"The controls and the organization of the race?" he wrote. "No car for me, just my bike. I was 26 years old and I was the champion of the cyclists' section at the Stade Français. So every stage I rode, I did my best to control the race. I followed the riders as far as the nearest station where the timetable would let me catch an express that would get me to the finish before the riders." On that opening day he took his first train to Moulins to watch the race pass, then another to Lyon.

Remember that the shortest stage was 268 km and the longest, from Paris to Lyon, a startling 467. Garin rode so fast — 26 km/h — that he reached the finish before the judges. "They are going faster than the train," Lefèvre wrote. The stint from Lyon, three days later, started at 2:30 a.m. And that was a luxury: in Marseille (10:30 p.m.) and Bordeaux (11.30 p.m.) they started the previous day.

Garin won the first stage, Aucouturier the next two. By Toulouse, Aucouturier had an easy lead. But he faded and Garin won, occasionally favored by officials who passed him food knowing that their boss wanted him to win.

Of one of his two assistants, the starter Abran, Lefèvre recalled: "His role was to wave an immense yellow flag at the start and at the finish and, hat askew, moustache bristling, his face bright red, to sit behind a Pernod at the race café." The other, Fernand Mercier, traveled ahead to arrange each stage's finish with *L'Auto*'s local correspondent.

The first Tour had begun. Those who dropped out could join in again for the day's prizes but not the final awards. Garin was two hours and 49 minutes ahead of the rest. The last man was two days and 16 hours in arrears. Nobody knew if there'd be another. But it was already a success for *L'Auto*. It had a special edition on the streets within seven minutes of the finish — an astonishing achievement even now — and they sold instantly. It printed 14,178,474 papers in 1903; by 1913 it was 43,641,875, or 120,000 a day. During the Tour of 1922, it was printing more than 600,000 a day. And on November 20, 1904, *Le Vélo* went out of business. Giffard's beak had been nailed shut.

5
Into the Mountains

THE SUFFERING in those first Tours was enormous. In 1998 I watched Marco Pantani ride the mountains like a sprinter, out of the saddle with his hands on the bottom of the bars, braking for the bends. It wasn't always so. Alan Gayfer stood at the top of one of those climbs as editor of *Cycling*. He got talking to an old man who'd been brought out for the day by his family.

> We chatted for a while and then, rather shyly, he said he'd ridden the Tour de France 40 years earlier. Well, that was in the 1960s, so it'd have been the 20s. I said the roads must have been very different, and he said "*Oui, monsieur*, they were very rough surfaces then."
>
> I pointed at the way the riders would be coming and said I'd seen the climb in the days of Bobet and Coppi, when there were holes in the surface and stones and rocks on the road. Now, of course, they're in a very good state, more or less smooth like any other road. And he looked very surprised and he said "*Non monsieur*, you don't understand. We didn't come up there!" And he turned and pointed at a tiny goat track behind us, all rocks and tufts of grass and no more than a few yards wide.
>
> "We came up that road there!"

The roads were "*épouvantable* [dreadful]," according to Roger Lapébie, who was a guest of the Tour in 1999 when a stage finished in Bordeaux, near his home. "There were potholes that we used to call birds' nests, pebbles, dust, gravel. We got lots of saddle sores because of the dirt, the cow dung. It was easy to get infected." He, like most, used mustard plasters at night. "American or English were best. We'd buy packets of three or four dozen in Paris and put them on our legs all night if they were painful. If the weather was bad, we'd put two on our liver, one on our front." Riders took salted baths every night, dosing the water with vinegar as well. They rubbed their legs with seaweed, he said.

The Tour's first major climb was the Ballon d'Alsace, in the Vosges mountains in the east. Eight miles of 10 percent gradient set off a debate — encouraged by Desgrange — about whether anybody could tackle such a climb except on foot. In fact the Ballon confirmed René Pottier as the Tour's first star climber as he hammered up the "unridable" mountain at 14 mph and crushed Cornet, the 1904 winner, three miles from the top. Pottier was the only rider to ride all the

The roads were terrible, said Roger Lapébie, with holes as big as bird's nests. The grand old man of the Tour, the first to win with a derailleur, is still honored by the race that never forgot him. Here, as guest of honor, he sits on the rostrum seats and waits for the winners at Bordeaux in 1999.

way, but it gave him tendinitis and he withdrew next morning. A year later he did it again and won the Tour.

Sadly, though, this strange man was consumed by demons. He never joked, he never laughed, he never told stories nor reminisced. A Peugeot mechanic found him six months later, on January 25, 1907, hanging from the hook that usually held his bike. His brother André blamed a broken heart, "sentimental disappointment." But René left no message and his death remains a mystery. There's a memorial to him at the top of the Ballon, and André broke down and retired when he reached it next summer.

But the Ballon was a one-off. The real climbs lay further south. Desgrange gets the credit now for sending riders over the mountains but at the time he dismissed the idea as crazy and it took several years to change his mind. The man who did it was Alphonse Steines, a dapper man with rimless glasses, a neat beard, and a *belle époque* moustache. Steines persuaded Desgrange that the Tour had grown dull and droned about it so much that eventually Desgrange sent him off in January 1910 to survey the Pyrénées.

January, of course, is midwinter. Steines looked at the Aubisque and paid for the repair of the road. But the Tourmalet is 2,114 m high and impossible to cross because of the snow. Steines returned just before the race, although the mountain was still snow-capped. The road across it was unsurfaced and Steines found it hard to persuade anybody to drive him. That was hardly surprising: only a week earlier a Mercedes had dropped into a ravine. When he did find a driver, a man called Dupont, his car ground to a halt in 12 feet of snow with two miles to go. It was 6 p.m. Steines, to Dupont's disbelief, got out and walked into the night in city clothes. He fell several times, got lost, and the police in Barèges had to send out a search party to bring him down and thaw him out. It was a disaster he kept from Desgrange.

"Crossed Tourmalet," he telegraphed. "Very good road. Perfectly practicable. Steines."

The papers knew nothing of this, nor that *L'Auto* had paid 2,000 francs to have part of the road repaired. But they wrote of "dangerous and weird" developments. Twenty-six big names immediately said they had no intention of riding. Lucien Petit-Breton protested: "It's murder... those bastards want our skin!" Gustave Garrigou said years afterwards: "No joke — people were telling us about avalanches, road collapses, of the killer mountains, and the Thunder of God!" Riders on reconnaissance in May claimed to have seen a bear. They got back to Luchon and told reporters: "Desgrange is sending us into a circle of death!"

They weren't far wrong. Desgrange — at Steines' suggestion — sent them over the Peyresourde, Aspin, Tourmalet and Aubisque, all on the unmade roads the old man showed to Gayfer. They were places where people feared to go by foot, let alone bike. Desgrange, delighted but still shy of his reputation, did what he did in 1903. He stayed at home. He said he was unwell. The Tour's own history says: "The organizers fear they have pushed the limits of human force and courage a little too far, to the point where they think the Pyrénées might be the Tour's last adventure. Under pressure, Desgranges [*sic*] cracks and quits."

Instead, he sent his deputy, Victor Breyer, and other officials. They reached the summit of the Aubisque with no idea how long it would take the riders and waited in the thin but unusually warm night air. The delay turned out longer than their worst guess and they grew

It's bleak and formidable even when the sun shines. But for Alphonse Steines, the night-time journey across a snow-covered Tourmalet nearly cost him his life. He fell in the snow and was found frozen and soaked. Nevertheless he cabled Desgrange to tell him the road was fine and that he could send his race. Half-close your eyes as you look at the picture and you can see why the coureurs feared bears and brigands would kill them if the gradient didn't.

worried. Perhaps tales of bears had been justified, or maybe there really were brigands in the hills. And what about the unguarded drops into the valley?

Down below, most pedaled when they could, but otherwise pushed their single-gear bikes. Only a local, François Lafourcade from Bayonne, rode all the way. The officials ran down to him. "What's happened? Where are the others? Are they behind you? Are they safe?"

Lafourcade, exhausted after four mountains, stared at them wordless and pressed on. More time passed. Maybe 15 minutes. A dust-covered figure appeared, slowly pushing his bike. It took an agony for Octave Lapize to reach the car. When he did, he turned to Breyer and the others and shouted "Murderers!" It became a legend of the Tour. "I'm quitting the race on the way down the mountain," he yelled, and he rode on. Lapize, known to his friends as *Frisé* (Curly), was more a sprinter than a climber, but his courage returned on the road to Bayonne and he won the stage. Then he beat the Giant of Colombes, François Faber, to win the Tour itself.

Lapize didn't live much longer. He died in 1917 as a fighter pilot at Verdun. Faber perished early as well, shot in the head during a Foreign Legion attack on Garency in May 1915 as he struggled from German lines with an injured colleague on his shoulders. And why the

Not the greatest sculpture in the world but a tribute nevertheless. These days there are cyclists on the Tourmalet all through the summer; at the beginning, though, riders walked and rode with eyes sunken into their sockets through exhaustion.

Foreign Legion? Because he was from Luxembourg, even though he lived at Colombes, near Paris.

He was no stranger to misery. He once broke his chain and ran a kilometer to the finish, pushing his bike. He won the astonishing Tour of 1909, when snow, rain, frost, wind, mud, lakes of puddles, and knee-deep ruts forced out 50 riders in a week. His mother turned out for the second stage, scared she'd bring him bad luck. She did. Freezing rain fell for all 398 km from Roubaix to Metz. Faber rode the last 200 km alone. Next day he rode another 100 km alone, covered in mud, including the near-freezing Ballon, and finished 33 minutes ahead of the next man overall. His manager, Baugé, called him "the god who came down to ride a bicycle."

Was that enough? No. The next day began at 2 a.m. Three thousand turned out to watch the start. Faber rode the 21 km col de Porte in an hour and ten minutes, despite strong wind, two falls, and being brought down by a horse that kicked his bike 30 feet away. The day brought potholes, knee-high water, and broken chains. Twenty thou-

They made them harder in those days: François Faber once ran a mile to the finish after his chain broke. They called him, with reason, the Giant of Colombes, after the area of Paris in which the Luxembourger lived. Sadly, like so many other stars of the time, he died in the First World War.

sand watched him ride alone into Lyon, many trying to touch him. His sheer size was impressive — a shade under 6 ft. 2 in. and weighing 91 kg (200 lbs.). He was cycling's gentle giant. Garrigou called him a phenomenon.

Desgrange rather liked being called a murderer, and so he included the Alps as well. He put the 2,646 m Galibier into the 1911 Tour, and again he excelled himself.

"Oh Laffrey! Oh Bayard! Oh Tourmalet!" he wrote. "I don't hesitate to proclaim that compared to the Galibier you are but pale and vulgar babies. In front of this giant there is nothing more for you to do but take off your hats and bow from down below." *L'Auto* reporters could now revel in even more titanic struggles through the hills and storms of hell. They didn't actually see much of it, of course, but then neither did those who bought the papers.

In 1937, *L'Auto* came across Garrigou in a general store in the rue Lepic. It didn't say it was Paris but there's a Passage Lepic off the boulevard de Clichy near Pigalle, so perhaps it was there. Garrigou was a classic climber, skinny as a broom, and a snappy dresser. He rode eight Tours from 1907 to 1914, finished them all, won one, came second three times, twice third, and also finished fourth and fifth.

He spoke of "summits that only the eagles could get to. *Oh la la!* The highest summits in Europe. That was the bad side, the bad roads... not even a road, just donkey tracks... and I'm being polite. It wasn't anything superhuman because we weren't supermen, and I'm the proof, a man like anybody else, with four Galibiers in my pocket, then the Tourmalet, where I won five Louis [sovereigns] because I climbed all the way up without walking."

They rode with canvas food bags on their handlebars, holes in the bottom to let the rain run out. Their goggles left white circles in the sweat-encrusted grime on their faces, and they carried spare tires looped figure-of-eight around their shoulders. The goggles, it's worth saying, weren't against the sun. They were against muck and stones and dust.

"It was our job," said Garrigou. "The prizes, the primes, the contracts. I was a professional. It was just life."

Misery in the Valley

DESGRANGE wasn't always personally responsible for the suffering. In 1920 Napoléon Paoli hit a donkey on the road to Bayonne, ended up on its back and galloped off back the way he'd come. He clung to it until it hurt its leg and collapsed. Then he let go, ran back to his bike and carried on racing, although with a sore stomach. All went well for a few moments, after which a rock fell from a cliff and hit him on the head. He struggled on until the start of the Tourmalet, but by then the pain was unbearable and he gave up and fell asleep in a hut.

Sometimes, though, Desgrange went out of his way to make things worse. Léon Scieur, from Floreffe in Belgium, was an unlucky sort of man: he once punctured a record eight times on a single stage. In 1921 he broke 11 spokes on the last-but-one stage, from Metz to Dunkirk, and managed to get another wheel. Unfortunately, he couldn't use it until the judges had seen the problem that made it necessary. Otherwise he had to make his own repair, which with 11 spokes was impossible. There'd been no judges around when they broke so he carried the wheel on his back for 300 km to Metz. The sprocket made a mark he still bore 15 years later.

A similar fate befell Eugène Christophe, a little Frenchman who once had a big moustache so like an ancient Gaul's that the press called him *Le Vieux Gaulois*, although his fans preferred "Cri-Cri." They loved him for his independence and his rugged looks, with widely spaced and hooded eyes above a firm, broad mouth and square jaw. These days he's known for the toe-clips that carry his name, but in 1913 he was a favorite for the Tour, which was circling France counterclockwise for the first time and back to being judged on time rather than points. Peugeot and Alcyon had each won four times and the tie-break was between Odile Defraye, Alcyon's winner the previous year, and Peugeot's 28-year-old runner-up, Christophe.

The battleground was the sixth stage from Bayonne to Luchon, including the Aubisque, Gourette, Soulor, Tourmalet, Aspin and Peyresourde. Peugeot attacked from the flag at 3 a.m. to demoralize Alcyon. It worked. Defraye was 11 minutes behind in Oloron-Sainte-Marie, 14 in Eaux-Bonnes, an hour in Argelès-Gazost on the other side of the Aubisque, and at the foot of the Tourmalet at Barèges he climbed off after 244 km. He was two hours behind Christophe and his team-mate Philippe Thys, who'd gone away on the Tourmalet. Years later, old and bandy, Christophe returned to the mountain, pointed into the mist-filled valley and told one of the Tour's most epic tales.

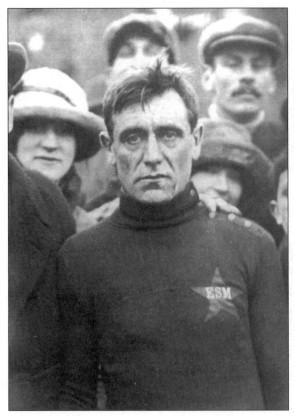

He looks unhappy, and well he might — Eugène Christophe was riddled by bad luck. He reveled in the mud and rain, so much that riders nicknamed him Hippopotamus. His giant moustache made him look like an old Gaulois but he was less recognizable when he shaved it off and it prompted the Tour to give him the first yellow jersey, so spectators would recognize him.

"All of a sudden, about ten kilometers from Sainte-Marie-de-Campan down in the valley, I felt that something is wrong with my handlebar. I pull on my brake and stop. I see my fork is broken. I can tell you now that my fork was broken, but I would not tell you at that time because it was bad advertising for my firm. So there I was, left alone on the road. When I say road, I should say the path. I thought that maybe one of these steep pack trails would lead me straight to Ste-Marie-de-Campan. But I was crying so badly I couldn't see anything. With my bike on my shoulder, I walked for all those ten kilometers.

"On arriving at the village I met a young girl who led me to the blacksmith on the other side of the village. Monsieur Lecomte was the name of the blacksmith. He was a nice man and wanted to help me, but he wasn't allowed to. The regulations were strict. I had to do all

Christophe broke his forks on the Tourmalet and spent hours in a forge repairing them, his penalty extended by asking a boy to pump the bellows. In his sixties, Christophe returned to the forge of Sainte-Marie-de-Campan to re-enact the drama of 1913

the repair myself. I never spent a more wretched time in my life than those cruel hours in M. Lecomte's forge."

Judges and rival team officials made sure he did the work himself. At one point Christophe realized the fire was getting low and, with one hand holding the hammer and the other the broken forks, allowed a seven-year-old boy called Corni to pump the flames with bellows. For that he was fined a further ten minutes, later reduced to three. Having already ridden across mountains since three that morning, walked six miles with a broken bike and spent three hours on its repair, Cri-Cri made it into Luchon on an uncertain and unsafe machine at 8:44 p.m. He was 29th, astonishingly beating 15 others. There's a plaque now on the wall of the house that stands where the forge once was, and Christophe and the small boy were there in 1951 to re-enact the incident and see it put in place. It's 400 meters out of the village on the right-hand side of the road to Campan. The small square in Ste-Marie-de-Campan is known now as the Place Eugène Christophe.

This is where Christophe arrived, lugging his broken bike and pursued by officials and villagers. The original forge has gone but the house stands on its site. You can find it by turning left at the foot of the Tourmalet and riding gently downhill for a few hundred meters. The house is on your right.

Astonishingly, history repeated itself. Christophe was leading the longest stage in 1919 — 468 km from Metz to Dunkirk. It was July 18, the last but one day. He rose to an attack by Firmin Lambot and his fork broke again on roads damaged by war. This time there was a small bicycle factory a mile away near Valenciennes but he still had to mend his bike alone. He lost two hours and dropped from first to tenth, or last but one because everybody else had given up. Readers of *L'Auto* sent money to bring his winnings to what they would have been. Finally, in 1922, he was again coming down a mountain — this time the Galibier — moving north on the D902 towards the Télégraphe, when he hit a block of stone. He got to Valloire, the nearest village, where the parson offered him a bike with rotten brakes.

"Take it," he said. "It's yours." Christophe declined. The Lord might look after a *curé* with bad brakes but his own record with God's fortunes wasn't so dependable.

"That accident didn't upset me as much as the others," Christophe said dryly. "By then I was a bit of an expert."

Another Frenchman, Victor Fontan, thought his career would end without riding the Tour, not least because he'd been shot twice in the leg in World War I. He came to racing late and he'd rarely competed outside south-west France, so when selectors finally picked him at 36 he was delighted. In 1929, near his home, he achieved the unthinkable when he took the yellow jersey in the Pyrénées. He set off in his *maillot jaune*, eager to impress neighbors who'd dismissed him as too old, and set a cracking pace on the 363 km to Luchon. Then he crashed and broke his forks.

It was the middle of the night, and Fontan set off in the moonlight to find a new bike. He came to a village and walked from house to house, hammering on doors and waking the residents. They blinked in the darkness, astonished to find the leader of the Tour de France on their doorstep, and eventually someone lent him a bike. He climbed on, pedaled into the night and regained some time. But it was too late. Disillusioned, he abandoned.

Of all misfortunes, however, one stands out. In 1951, 12 days into the race, Wim van Est became the first Dutchman to wear the yellow jersey. I first met him in the 1970s at one of those criteriums that dot southern Holland. He was a friend's uncle, as barrel-shaped as ever, dressed in a cardigan and looking for all the world as if he'd just been tending his vegetables. Much later I spent an evening at his home in St

Willebrord, near the Belgian border. He talked with one hand on a cigarette, which he said he didn't inhale, and an eye on soccer on television.

"That day," he told me, "I was away with a group of 13, 14 riders. And there was a really fast rider with us, Louis Caput, a Frenchman. Good sprinter. He attacked a kilometer from the line but we got him back. But when we got to the track, it was an old ash track, a horse-racing track, and on a track like that I was unbeatable. I raced on that sort of finish so often. And I won and I took the yellow jersey."

There were several cols between Dax and Tarbes next day, and van Est, never a climber, wasn't looking forward to them. They went over the Soulor, took the little drop to the foot of the Aubisque, and started climbing again.

> There were nine or ten men away and we were gritting our teeth to get them back, and then in the first bend of the descent there were just Stan Ockers and Fausto Coppi, a few hundred meters in front of us. Well, that first bend was wet, slippery from the snow. And there were sharp stones

Fig. 6.4. The French cycling association placed this plaque on the wall where the forge once stood. "Here in 1913," it says, "Eugène Christophe, French racing cyclist, leader of the Tour de France, victim of an accident to his machine on the Tourmalet, repaired his bicycle fork at the forge. Despite having walked numerous kilometers on the mountain, and lost several hours, Eugène Cristophe (note the misspelling) would not abandon the challenge that he would have won, showing an example of supreme willpower."

on the road that the cars had kicked up and my front wheel hit them and I went over.

There was a drop of 20 meters. They've built a barrier round it now but then there was nothing to stop you going over. I fell 20 meters, rolling and rolling and rolling. My feet had come out of the straps, my bike had disappeared, and there was a little flat area, the only one that's there, no bigger than the seat of a chair, and I landed on my backside.

A meter left or right and I'd have dropped on to solid stone, six or seven hundred meters down. My ankles were all hurt, my elbows were *kaput*. I was all bruised and shaken up and I didn't know where I was, but nothing was broken. I just lay there. And the other riders were going by, I could see. And then right at the top I could make out my team-mate, Gerrit Peeters, looking down at me.

You looked just like a buttercup down there," he told me afterwards, with the yellow jersey on, you know.

The Dutch manager, Kees Pellenaars, brought the team car to the edge and threw down a rope, but it was too short.

They got 40 tubulars, knotted them together, tied them to the tow rope, and threw it down to me. It was all the tyres that Pellenaars had for the team. By the time they'd tugged me up, all the tubs were stretched and they wouldn't stay on the wheels any more. Forty tubs! I wanted to get on my bike and start riding again. One of the journalists gave me a flask of cognac, and I was saying "I want to go on, I want to go on." But I couldn't. Pellenaars stopped the whole team. "We'll be back next year," he said. It was good publicity. I got home and the whole neighborhood was out to greet me.

A Swiss watch company signed van Est for an advertisement. It showed him battered from his fall... and carried the legend "My heart stopped, but not my Pontiac."

7
Dubious Cases

IF THE MOUNTAINS, the distance, the early starts weren't enough, Desgrange could always add extra rules to take such happiness that remained in his riders' lives. His keenness for lawmaking sometimes exceeded his interest in the race. Henri Alavoine more than once made up for poor climbing by striking up an argument about some minor injustice. Desgrange became too engrossed to notice that Alavoine spent mile after mile clinging to his car. Not that Alavoine was a slacker. He finished the last six miles of the 1909 Tour carrying his bike on his shoulder.

Desgrange liked to speak of the divine bicycle "and the indescribable and precious joy that it brings." At the same time he made sure it was otherwise. The most notorious example involved the Pélissier brothers, Francis and Henri. Henri was a barrack-room lawyer and much of what he said was justified. Tour riders, after all, were allowed only to ride and sleep. They had no other rights. But he also had a big mouth. After winning a stage and coming second in two others, he gloated: "The others are cart horses; I'm a thoroughbred." The cart horses took exception. Next day Pélissier flatted and the whole field shot off like startled starlings, leaving Henri and Francis to struggle 30 minutes behind.

Desgrange had a niggling rule that a rider could finish the day with neither more nor less than he started. He'd penalized Pélissier two minutes for leaving a flat tire by the roadside in 1920 and Henri, the shop steward, left the race in protest. Pélissier then won race after race everywhere else but stayed away from the Tour.

"Pélissier can win any race except the Tour," Desgrange scoffed, and Pélissier was stung, just as Desgrange knew he would be, and he returned in 1923 to win. But neither he nor Desgrange had changed. The second stage of 1924 started cold and Pélissier wore two jerseys, throwing away the first as the day warmed up. A clash between the autocrat and what he called "this pigheadedly arrogant champion" was inevitable.

Further down the road, the journalist Albert Londres was waiting to see the French favorites pass. When they didn't, he wrote a piece called "Les Forçats de la Route" for *Le Petit Parisien*, some of the most atmospheric writing the Tour has produced. The title can be translated as the convicts — or the chain-gang, the forced laborers — of the road:

That morning, we went on ahead of the bunch. We were at Granville and six o'clock was sounding. Some riders arrived and the crowd, feeling confident, cried "Henri!... Francis!"

Henri and Francis weren't among them. We waited.

The second category riders passed — the dark ones. The dark ones were the *touriste-routiers*, the courageous little guys who belonged to no big bicycle factory, those who had no tires but fire in their belly — neither Henri nor Francis appeared.

The new cry then was "The Pélissiers have abandoned."

We return to the Renault and, without a care for our tires, we went back to Cherbourg. The Pélissiers are worth a set of tires.

Coutances. A bunch of kids are talking about what's happened.

"Have you seen the Pélissiers?"

"Seen them? I could have touched them," says one snot-nose.

"You know where they are?"

"At the bar at the station. Everybody's there."

Everybody was there. We had to use our elbows to get into the bistro. The crowd was silent. They said nothing, just looked spellbound into the distance. Three jerseys were sitting at the front of the table in front of three bowls of hot chocolate. It's Henri, Francis, and the third is none other than the second, meaning Maurice Ville, who came second at Le Havre and at Cherbourg.

"Had a bang?"

"No," says Henri. "It's just that we're not dogs."

"What's happened?"

"A question of jerseys. This morning at Cherbourg, the commissaire approached me and, without saying anything, he lifted my jersey. He was checking that I didn't have two jerseys. What would you say if I lifted your jacket to see if you had a white shirt? I don't like his manners. That's all."

"What would have happened if you'd had two jerseys?"

"I could have had 15, but I don't have the right to leave with two and finish with only one."

"Why?"

"It's the rule. It's not enough that we should race like brutes, we also have to freeze or stifle. That's all part of the sport as well, it seems. Well, I went to find Desgrange."

"I haven't got the right to throw my jersey on the road, then?"

"No, you can't throw away Tour property."

"It's not Tour property, it's mine."

"I will not hold discussions in the street."

"If you won't discuss it in the street, I'm going back to bed.'"

"We'll sort it out in Brest."

"That can all be sorted out in Brest because I'm washing my hands of it." And I washed my hands of it.

The brothers Pélissier live on in bas-relief. Their faces watch over the entrance of the Piste Municipale in western Paris, where the Tour finished for some years after the Parc des Princes and before the Champs Elysées. French cyclists were so impressed by their heroes that they clubbed together to buy the sculpture for the Parc des Princes. It was moved here when the Parc was demolished.

"I rejoined the bunch and I said, 'Come on, Francis, we're chucking it in.'"

"And that sounded fine to me," said Francis, "because just this morning I'd had a bad stomach."

"And you, Ville?"

"Me?" Ville replied, laughing like a big baby. "They picked me up on the roadside. I had painful knees."

The Pélissiers don't only have legs but heads as well. And in those heads, judgment.

"You have no idea what the Tour de France is," says Henri. "It's a calvary. What's more, the path of the cross only has 14 stations, whereas ours

The Tour could cross the mountains only once cars had become as reliable as the riders. Here, Fontan and Frantz fight it out on the Tourmalet. The rider by the roadside has no bottles and is probably a spectator. But look closely at the man next to the car. His right hand looks suspiciously as though it's hanging on to the car.

has 15. We suffer on the road. But do you want to see how we keep going? Wait..."

He gets a phial from his bag.

"That, that's cocaine for our eyes, and chloroform for our gums..."

"That," says Ville, emptying his shoulder-bag, "that's horse ointment to warm my knees."

"And pills? You want to see the pills?"

They get out three boxes apiece.

"In short," says Francis, "we run on dynamite."

Henri continues: "Have you seen us in the bath at the finish? Make an appearance. Take away the mud and we're as white as shrouds. Diarrhoea empties us. In the evenings, in our rooms, we dance a jig like Saint Vitus instead of sleeping...

"Look at our laces. Well, they don't go on for ever. They break, and they're made of tanned leather, at least I imagine.

"Think what happens to our skin...

"And the nails of our feet," says Henri. "I've lost six out of ten. They fall off little by little every stage. And, well! Wait for the Pyrénées. It's hard labor. All that we get paid for. Unless it can be done only by mules, we'll do it. We're not slackers. But, in the name of God, don't harass us. We accept the torment but we don't want vexations. My name is Pélissier, not Atlas. If I have a newspaper on my chest when I leave, I have to have it when I finish. If not, a penalty. To drink, I have to do the pumping myself. The day will come when they'll put lead in our pockets, because they'll claim that God has made men too light."

It's a great snapshot of drama and discontent on the road, but there's a twist. Londres was a celebrated writer but no sports specialist. He was writing for color. Francis Pélissier eventually became manager of the La Perle team and he said of that day at Coutances: "Londres was a famous reporter but he didn't know much about cycling. We kidded him a bit with our cocaine and our pills. Even so, the Tour de France in 1924 was no picnic." Was even that the truth, or just the recollections of a rebel who'd joined the establishment?

The brothers, three of whom held the yellow jersey, grew up in Paris's poshest suburb. Henri, Jean, Francis, and Charles were regulars at the Buffalo track and the training circuits of the Bois de Boulogne to the west of the city. Francis was *le Grand* because of his height and he went on to manage an emerging 18-year-old called

Jacques Anquetil. Dandy Charles was called Brummel, after Beau Brummel, and Jean died in the First World War.

They never liked the Tour and its mishaps. Henri won in 1923 and also the Tour of Lombardy three times and Paris–Roubaix twice. Francis won Bordeaux–Paris twice and Charles was French cyclo-cross champion three times. But Henri came to an unhappy end, mentally ill. Léonie, his first wife, shot herself in despair in 1933. Then his mistress, Camille Tharault, 20 years his younger, used the same revolver to shoot him five times at their home at Fourcherolles outside Paris in May 1935.

Henri loved her and called her *Miette*, but they had lengthy rows and he'd been threatening her with a knife. A bullet hit his carotid artery and blood spurted everywhere. The shock to France was enormous. He'd been retired eight years, but he was still a national hero; the French federation president called him the greatest rider of all time. Camille pleaded self-defense and on May 26, 1936, she got a year's suspended jail sentence.

There are still those in France who wish another Henri Pélissier could return from the dead.

8
... And Cheats

WHETHER the Pélissiers were exaggerating or not, drugs have been part of cycling since the start. A rider died of them in the 19th century and the old six-day races were a den of drugs as competitors rode until they collapsed. Trainers dropped cocaine on their tongues or massaged it into their legs with butter. A spectator unfamiliar with the misery asked why a rider kept ducking each lap.

"The fool thinks there's a bridge there," was the reply.

The Belgian star Rik van Steenbergen wrote in a Brussels paper in 1967: "Sometimes I had to ride in Paris and then immediately after the race get into my car and drive for ten hours to Stuttgart, where I was back on my bike again. Things like that happened every week. There was nothing you could do. An organizer wanted this star and that star on his bill and he paid handsomely for it. Another organizer wanted those same stars a day later... The top riders were obliged to be fresh each time and they couldn't do that without stimulants. Nobody could or ever will be able to do that because there are no such things as supermen. Doping is necessary in cycling."

The journalist Willem van Wijnendaele wrote in 1954 of a pursuiter who "was in a shocking state before his ride against the general favorite... His feverish eyes were deep into his face and he kept licking his dry lips as though he had a thirst but nothing to help it. They were sure signs [of amphetamine doping] that no doctor could mistake, and we all knew he had taken something. I pointed him out to several colleagues and in no time there was a crowd of soigneurs, journalists, and managers, all having a look. Somebody shouted 'Nobody smoke in case there's an explosion!'"

Tony Hewson, one of the first English-speakers to make a living at cycling in Europe after the war, told Richard Yates in *On The Wheel*: "Most riders I knew made selective use of amphetamine stimulants that you could buy freely over the counter of any chemist shop [pharmacy], so-called pep-pills, sometimes mixing them with sherry or strong coffee to enhance the effect."

Kees Pellenaars, who pulled van Est from the Aubisque, tells in his autobiography, *Daar was 't*, of a rider in one of his teams:

> I took him along to a training camp in Spain. The boy changed then into a sort of lion. He raced as though he was powered by rockets... I went to talk to him. He was really happy that he was riding so well, and he told me to look out for him. I asked him if he wasn't perhaps "using something" and he jumped straight up, climbed on a chair, and from deep inside a closet pulled out a plastic bag of pills.
>
> I felt my heart skip a beat. I had never seen so many fireworks together. With a soigneur and another rider, we counted the pills. There were five thousand of them, excluding hormone preparations and sleeping pills. I took the five thousand bombs away, to his own relief. I let him keep the hormones and the sleeping pills. Later he seemed to have taken too many at once and he slept for a couple of days on end. We couldn't wake him up. We took him to hospital and they pumped out his stomach. They tied him to his bed to prevent anything going wrong again. But somehow he had some stimulant and fancied taking a walk. A nurse came across him in the corridor, walking along with the bed strapped to his back.

The French manager Marcel Bidot said, "Three-quarters of the riders are doped. I am well placed to know since I visit their rooms each evening during the Tour. I always leave frightened after these visits." The Tour doctor Pierre Dumas spoke of "medicine from the heart of Africa... healers laying on hands or giving out irradiating balms, feet plunged into unbelievable mixtures that could lead to eczema, so-called magnetized diets, and everything else you could imagine." Even riders worried. For some years the Tour was shadowed by a semipro version called the Tour de l'Avenir. One French rider was in such a state that others pushed him off his bike for his own safety.

Doctors found him foaming at the roadside. Even his manager insisted on a drug test, predictably positive.

The Dutch rider Theo Sijthoff told Theo Koomen, in *25 Jaar Doping*, how a colleague asked him if he'd "prepared:"

I showed him my bike and let him check my tires. To my surprise he shook his head. He didn't mean that at all. He meant whether I had taken anything.

"How do you mean, taken?"

"Good Lord," he said. He took me along to his cabin and opened a case.

"What do you think?" he asked. It looked just like a chemist's shop. Pills, powders, everything.

"Here," he said. "Stenamine," I read.

"Take it."

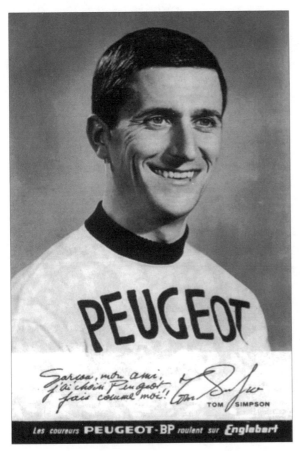

"Hey pal, I chose a Peugeot," Tom Simpson wrote on this publicity picture. "Do the same as I." In 1967 Simpson's white Peugeot fell to the roadside on Mont Ventoux, its straps still wrapped round his feet. He was dying as he hit the white stones and melting tar of the old volcano. His death, with drugs in his pockets and body, marked the beginning of the end and the start of a new era for the Tour.

I swallowed and in a flash I was in heaven. I felt I could fly. I only had to stick out my wings and I'd be away. I rode fantastically. If doctors say now that that stuff doesn't do anything, I just have to laugh... The spectators were really enthusiastic and I got a contract for fifteen races.

Stenamine, that was the stuff. I had only heard of it as an amateur. Pros had to prepare themselves that way. I bought a small case and I crammed a whole apothecary in it. Methedrin, best stuff, dexedrine, Pervitin, a still stronger goody called Maxiton.

Another recalled: "Just before a race, riders were unrecognizable from a couple of hours earlier... What are we having today? Methidrin? Hoorah! We injected ourselves without a thought for hygiene; 15mg in the right thigh, 15 mg in the left thigh, 10 mg of ephedrine to breathe better in the backside and another dose of solucamphor to soften the muscles. That was nice. Except you couldn't sleep at night. Hours on end you stared at the ceiling in the hotel or at home with your wife. That's how it is with the Guild of Ceiling Starers."

He wasn't unusual. Dutch doctors said in 1961 that "from the data we gathered... there is hardly a racing cyclist (professional, amateur, or junior) who does not use doping." Things became embarrassing. Dumas presented evidence that said, "I have seen slobbering cyclists on the roadside, their mouths foaming. Ill-tempered, they kick their bikes to smash them, making disordered gesticulations. Another hits his head with a bottle of mineral water he has just been given. Yet another throws himself at a barrier and breaks it... What can be said of a rider who, in a straight line and on a road 20 meters wide, leaves the road and crashes into a barrier... and this only a short while after putting his hand into his pocket for a *petit bidon?*"

Two incidents accentuated the problem. The first involved Knut Enemark Jensen, one of Denmark's team for the 100 km time-trial at the Rome Olympics. He began weaving and then sprawled across the road. The autopsy at Santa Eugenio hospital showed he'd taken Ronicol, or nicotinyl tartrate, which dilates the veins. The second, which really forced the sport's hand, was the death of the Briton Tom Simpson.

Professional cycling in the 1960s was predominantly French, Italian, and Belgian. Rules limited the places for foreign riders and there were no teams outside mainland Europe. The pressure on foreigners, therefore, was all the greater. They had to be good merely to get a place. The pressure to take drugs was enormous. More, Simpson had never been a convincing stage-race rider, courageous in one-day races but weedy.

"We always used to tease him in the showers about his hollow chest," said Vin Denson, his closest friend and team-mate in the fatal 1967 Tour.

Few English-speaking riders had done well, let alone held the yellow jersey. Shay Elliott of Ireland wore it between Jambes and Roubaix in 1963 and kept it for three days, and he came second to his brother-in-law, the Frenchman Jean Stablinski, in the 1962 world championship at Salo in Italy. And Simpson rode into yellow for a day across the Pyrénées between Pau and St.-Gaudens in 1962.

On July 13, 1967, the Tour was in Marseille. The 120 left in the race were by the harbor, preparing to ride over Mont Ventoux to Carpentras. Simpson was having trouble with his sponsor, Peugeot, and he was grateful that 1967 was for national rather than trade teams. He wouldn't have the support but nor would he have to fight for leadership. His plan was to earn what he could, invest $80,000, and retire.

The original plan to put a stained-glass window in the church of Simpson's home town in England proved too expensive. The money that British cyclists collected, though, was plenty enough for a memorial on the spot he fell. After 30 years it's starting to look chipped and shabby but riders still cross themselves as they pass and leave flowers.

He owned property in Belgium, where he lived, and he was optimistic enough to buy a new car and leave it in Ghent with his wife Helen so he could drive it after he'd come home by train from the Tour.

The Ventoux can be climbed in different directions. This time it was 10 miles of 10 percent gradient, first through trees and then the lava field to the observatory at the summit. Mont Ventoux is one of the worst climbs in the Tour. According to Alan Gayfer, "there was no question that Tom was afraid of the Ventoux. Everybody is afraid of the Ventoux. Eddy Merckx himself was afraid of the Ventoux. They know the Ventoux is an extremely tough mountain to climb; that's why they climb it."

It's not that its 1,900 m are the highest, more that the climb starts near sea level, temperatures rise with height, and there's little chance to recover. The Swiss Ferdy Kübler — Simpson called him Uncle Ferdy because their generous noses were so similar — planned to attack on it in 1955. France's Raphaël Géminiani warned him that "it's not a climb like the others." To which Kübler, not an easy speaker of French, answered: *"Ferdy aussi coureur pas comme les autres. Ferdy grand champion gagner à Avignon."* He attacked six miles from the top, followed by Louison Bobet and Géminiani himself. He became delirious, started weaving, crashed several times on the descent, and left the race next day.

In 1967 the heat was said to have been enough to burst the thermometer at Châlet Reynard — Bernard Bebière and Roger Viau's café halfway up. The tar was running in rivulets. Simpson was one of the first out of the trees and had ridden within sight of the observatory. He weakened suddenly and five riders passed him. He kept pedaling for a mile in the grey, lunar landscape. His team-mate, Colin Lewis, told me: "Nobody who wasn't there that day can imagine how hot it was."

And then he started "riding like an amateur" as his mechanic put it, weaving from the rubble on the right to the sheer drop on the left. His white Peugeot ran into loose stones at the foot of the bank and stopped. Simpson toppled on to his right shoulder, which carried a small Union Jack to identify his team. Harry Hall, a bike-shop owner in Manchester and one of the team's mechanics, undid his straps and told him he'd had enough. Simpson, still lucid, said "Get me up, get me up. I want to go on. Get me up, get me straight." Hall and the manager, the Anglo-Belgian Alec Taylor, pushed him up the hill, Hall scrambling to tighten the straps again. Taylor said he worried only that Simpson would take risks on the descent to make up time.

"For God's sake concentrate," Taylor shouted, and Simpson pressed on for another 300 meters. A UPI photographer wired off a picture with the caption that Simpson had died. Asked how he could write that of a man still on his bike, he said, "I saw it when I passed; death was in his face."

Simpson regained his rhythm but zigzagged again a kilometer from the summit. He collapsed, still strapped to his pedals. And there he died, despite mouth-to-mouth from Hall and oxygen from Pierre Dumas. His jersey was emptied of three small tubes after the helicopter got him to hospital in Avignon. Two were empty. The third held Stenamine and Tonedron, amphetamines. More were found in Simpson's luggage that evening. The inquest also showed Simpson had been drinking alcohol — Hewson, remember, said mixing amphetamine with sherry increased the effect — and Raymond Poulidor recalled that Simpson had stopped at a bar at the foot of the Ventoux with the Frenchman Jean-Pierre Genet.

The verdict was that he died of exhaustion and heat, exacerbated by altitude and drugs. He had taken enough, said the medical report, "to pass the limit of his endurance and so fall victim to excessive exhaustion." Tour organizer Jacques Goddet added: "We often asked ourselves whether he had committed some error in his manner of preparation."

Poulidor, recognizing both the heart failure and the drug aspect, said much later: "It was Simpson's death that triggered it [drug scandals] off, but in 1999 Simpson wouldn't be dead. He wouldn't have been allowed to start. In those days you just visited the doctor, he asked whether you were healthy, you just had to say yes, blow into the machine, and you were away! You were good for service."

A rider told me: "We didn't have the knowledge then; we just did not know what we were taking, that they were drugs."

It seemed unlikely.

"No, honestly," he said.

"So you never read the papers?"

"Of course I did."

"And you never noticed the fuss about national laws, not just cycling laws, about taking drugs in sport?"

There was no answer. This was 1967. The Tour had had nominal tests since 1965, and France published its first anti-doping law in November 1964. It seems unlikely that professional riders could have missed it. It was their job to know these things. The former pro Erwann Menthéour said in his book *Secret Défonce* [Secret High] in 1999 that riders pass their time in the evenings talking of just two things — girls and drugs — and it's hard to imagine it was much different 30 years earlier. The law was known well enough that some riders, particularly Jacques Anquetil, campaigned against its "unfairness." Cyclists should be as free to alleviate their suffering as a teacher with a headache, he said.

The Dutch journalist Jean Nelissen, who studied drug-taking for many decades, said, "In the business, it was accepted that the big champions knew precisely what they were doing. In the closing stages of a race they'd take 10 to 15 mg of preparations such as Tonedrin, Maxetonforte, or Pervitine. They were relatively modest doses. Everyone knows that a larger dose needs much more time for the stimulation to die. Who would risk taking too big a dose during a Tour de France and interrupting his night's rest? That was always a factor that limited the excess use of amphetamines."

Pierre Chany told how Anquetil and the Italian pursuiter and roadman Ercole Baldini met before the Grand Prix de Forli time-trial:

> They were the two favorites. They had a lot of admiration for each other. Anyway, that evening they were dining together with me and a few other close friends. I can't remember which of them said it but one turned to the other and said "You know what? We both know we're the favorites and that one or the other of us is going to win. Let's not bother with *l'amphet* [amphetamine]. Tomorrow, just to see, let's ride on just mineral water."
>
> The other agreed and they went off to bed. The next day, because they were both men of their word, they rode on mineral water. They certainly took the first two places, but they suffered like the damned to get an average speed that was a kilometer and a half an hour slower than they'd normally have ridden. "Never again!" they told me as they got off their bikes.

Still more extraordinary is the tale of July 28, 1950, a summer so hot that the bunch drove the organizers to fury by running off into the sea to cool off. The Tour was going from Perpignan to Nîmes, an uncomfortably hot ride for Europeans but not for two North Africans who'd made no mark on the race and were destined never to be heard of again. With 200 km to go, Marcel Molines and Abdel-Khader Zaaf bowled off together, getting up 20 minutes — enough to make Zaaf maillot jaune on the road. Suddenly Zaaf began weaving across the road with 12 miles to go, and an official pulled him off his bike. Zaaf tried again, staggered still more dramatically, and eventually fell asleep under a tree. Molines went on to win in Nîmes.

Under the tree, Zaaf came round, stared in alarm at the crowd, got back on his bike and rode off the wrong way. Spectators called an ambulance. Legend says he'd been revived with red wine, which Zaaf, a Muslim, had never tasted. Less charitable reports speak of drugs, heat, dehydration, and confusion. Red wine is an appealing story but it's scarcely likely he'd overcome a lifetime's religious conviction and down enough to make him drunk. But whatever, he was hugely upset and asked to ride the missing 12 miles before the next stage. Officials refused.

The occasion made Zaaf a celebrity. His start money rose from 200 to 2,000 francs. And then he vanished. He became just another legend of the Tour, a "whatever happened to..." And then on January 27, 1982, an old man came shuffling through a train station in Paris. A fan recognized him and the story began to unwind. One night in 1950, a soldier had knocked at Zaaf's door in Algeria, demanding his papers. Zaaf said he had only just come back from France, that he was too tired to go to the police station. As he closed the door, the soldier shot him in the leg.

In hospital he was left unseen until morning, then thrown into Baroughia jail for two years without trial, suspected of smuggling between Algeria and France. He lost all he owned except some hidden money. Prison diabetes damaged his sight and he'd come to Paris for an operation. France has a complex about the Algerian war, which killed thousands as two sides fought a complicated issue of independence with outrages on both sides, and again it warmed to the curious African who rode the wrong way. They sent him telegrams, flowers, and presents. He died in Algeria four years later, hero of the Tour's blackest comedy.

9
Teams and Donkeys

TACTICS played no part when the Tour began in 1903. You could watch a rider pass and cook a meal before the next turned up. Riders may have been individually sponsored, but teams — collections of riders with the same backer — began only the following year. The first were La Française, comprising Maurice Garin, his brother César, and Lucien Pothier, the runner-up in 1903, and Peugeot, led by Aucouturier.

Groupé riders had sponsors and kept themselves apart. The rules insisted on it. They couldn't ride with unsponsored *isolés* and Desgrange discouraged them from socializing or from sleeping in the same room. But while gaps reduced, and small groups established, the Tour was still more like a running race, the best challenging the rest to keep up.

Derailleurs made the Tour faster. The higher the speed, the more important to ride in a group, to ride "on a wheel." Teams employed stars and then others to lend their bodies — literally — in their service. Two stars could be too many, but in time there was room for a climber and a sprinter, neither of whom could challenge the leader. A cartoon in *Cycling* once showed a self-adoring star gazing into a mirror, his jersey labeled *"le perfect fit,"* another arrow pointing to *"les legs bronze."* A rider with ape-like arms and narrow brow was named *"le tough-guy sprinter,"* a spindly man *"le eagle,"* after Federico Bahamontes, the Eagle of Toledo, and then downbeat, muscle-weary, stupid-looking also-rans tagged as *"les domestiques, les controversial feature writers."*

Many were delighted to be domestiques, to be anything at all to be honest. They were given their day to win a race and, while they never earned much, good ones were sure of a living as the star took them from team to team. Desgrange coined the word domestique as an insult after the Parisian Maurice Brocco sold his services to others. "He is unworthy," Desgrange said, "he is a domestic [servant]." Brocco was stung and next day finished 21 minutes in front of Garrigou. That, he hoped, would put him back in Desgrange's good books. But not so. Desgrange contrasted the victory to his other performances and concluded he must surely have sold his help on other days.

"He deserves his punishment," he wrote. "Immediate disqualification."

Haunted and hunted, tin bottles stoppered with cork, dust goggles ready on his hat... another star of the old Tour rides past. Note the eyes white against sun-blackened skin and the lines of exhaustion beneath his eyes, the thin arms stripped of surplus cover by the endless hours of pedaling.

Once, riding from the Dutch border to Ostend, I sat in a bar between Ghent and Bruges and noticed an old picture of a man in a lettered jersey.

"Bent u dat?" I asked the man behind the bar — "Is that you?."

"Ja, lang geleden, meneer, zeker," he said — "Yes, sure, a long time ago." He laughed and said there were bars like his all over Belgium. "It doesn't seem much these days. Anybody with a few thousand francs can have a bar. But in the 1950s you were somebody with your own business, any business. I would've worked in the fields if I wasn't a *renner.* That's why we did it. You would share some of the prizes and get a wage and then maybe one day you would win a small race or even a day in the Tour.

"If you could win a stage, your name was made. You could ask much, much more and you were a hero in Belgium. Riders would dream of winning a stage. It could set them up in life, maybe open a bar or a garage. Me, I never did."

Riders had realizable ambitions, even Tour winners. The 1947 winner Jean Robic had a bar near the Gare Montparnasse in Paris; the Belgian world champion Stan Ockers kept one in the Gemeentestraat in Antwerp, where his trophies stood behind the bar and pictures on the walls showed him with Rik van Steenbergen after a six-day, and scenes from the Flèche Wallonne and the 1955 world championship.

Britain's Vin Denson — he had a bar in Ghent — was a donkey for Rik van Looy. He recalled: "You did whatever he wanted, including the fetching of beers, which he had a great fondness for in mid-race. Domestiques were reduced to chasing long miles to bring the great man a bottle of Stella." Denson learned of the Emperor's thirst when van Looy shouted *"Denson... café, café!"* He dropped off at the next café, filled his bottle and chased for miles. He fought back to the peloton and passed over the bottle. The Belgian felt its warmth, sniffed the lid, grimaced and emptied the contents on the road. Denson, not yet a pub owner, learned that day that *café* can mean bar as well as coffee.

Whether he paid for van Looy's coffee I have no idea. Possibly not. There was a tradition of stopping at cafés and raiding the shelves and refrigerator. Legend said patrons were delighted to have the stars — or more usually the also-rans — rob their stock. They were pictured watching with smiles. And well they might, since next day they sent a bill to the Tour, which must have been surprised how much beer could be stolen from even a small café.

The team system ended the brilliant individuality that the Tour encouraged. The Baron Pepin de Gontaud of Toulouse took Jean Dargassies and Henri Gauban to pace him in 1911. They proceeded at dignified pace and stayed in good hotels. For the first four stages, anyway, after which the baron decided he'd had a lovely if tiring time and would no longer ask the timekeepers to wait for him. At one time he was half a day behind the stage winner. The little party rode to the station, the baron gave more money to the three of them (they'd collected a third after pulling him exhausted from a ditch) than they could have won by finishing, and they parted company.

There were others. Marcel Dozol used to hand out photographs of himself. An 18-year-old Tunisian, Ali Neffati, rode in 1913 after apparently buying a bike only the previous afternoon. He was a delight to reporters and photographers in his red fez and complained of the cold while everyone else was sweating. Desgrange gave him a job at *L'Auto*, and he was said to have still been there in the 1950s after it had become *L'Équipe*.

The British *Daily Star* once sent a reporter to "join in that Tour de France and say what it's like." But once you really could. Touriste-routiers — the "dark ones" that Albert Londres mentioned — could

The Tour is officially part of France's inheritance, as recognized as the Eiffel Tower and the Palace of Versailles. Fifty years after Garin set off from Montgeron, the French post office issued a stamp commemorating half a century of extreme and ecstasy. The modern rider on the right is anonymous but the wide moustache of the ancien identifies him as Garin.

turn up from 1909 to 1938 if they took the entire organization on their shoulders. They slept outdoors if there were no hotels or sympathetic townsfolk. They put their suitcases on the train. Some did well. Mario Vicini of Italy finished second in 1937, 7:17 behind Roger Lapébie, and sixth in 1938. Ambrogio Morelli won stages in Pau and Caen in 1935 and came second overall, 17:52 behind Romain Maes of Belgium. They were rugged types changing one hardship for another. They could work 10 hours a day in a factory and longer in the fields or do the same on a bike with the chance of a decade's earnings in a summer. They picked the bike.

They followed training régimes considered a science at the time but proven to be nonsense with the passage of time. There were charming customs like wearing a cabbage leaf beneath a cap to fend off the sun and riding on a slice of steak to take the pressure off a saddle boil. They left their bikes untouched from November to January in the belief that their bodies would collapse from 12 months' riding, then trained with towels round their waist to sweat off fat. It was called "getting off the rough." One rider recalled winter sessions of 230 miles, all on fixed wheel: "The last 30 miles were virtually done in an insensitive daze, but since the big boys did this, you didn't question why."

There were other self-imposed hardships. Don't drink during a race, they said. If you want to win a race, give your water to a rival. The bottles in wire cages on the handlebars were for sipping only. Barrels of water were left at the finish for riders to slurp greedily and some of the sport's greatest miseries came from dehydration. Riders knew it and expected it, considered it part of their hardness. Marcel Kint, the world champion in 1938, was said to have trained on the wet roads of Flanders and eaten salted fish to get used to the thirst of the south of France. Times have changed; the odd thing is to think that the scientific training of 2000 and beyond may well be considered cranky and improbable in just 50 years' time.

10
Yellow Peril

SOME THINGS came early to the Tour. It took only three years to introduce the *flambe rouge*, for example, the red triangle that marks the last kilometer. But it took 16 years — until 1919 — to acquire the symbol by which the race is known all over the world.

It hadn't been easy for journalists and officials to identify the leader. Nor did it help *L'Auto*'s readers if their hero was just another dusty figure bent to the road. Something was needed. The idea came on a rest day between the 10th and 11th stages: the leader could wear a yellow jersey. The idea, legend insists, came from the journalists and officials themselves, and that seems likely given that Desgrange didn't often come up with worthwhile novelties of his own. Legend also says that Desgrange chose a yellow jersey because it was the color of *L'Auto*'s newsprint. Another version says he went into a bike shop and found that yellow was the only color available, which suited him because of its connections to his paper. But then again, unless the Tour in those less hygienic days was content to have just one jersey for the whole race regardless of dirt and tears, it seems improbable that even today a single shop would have enough jerseys of the same color to satisfy a big stage race.

Another, more likely, version is that Desgrange liked the idea of a leaders' jersey and called a manufacturer in Paris to make them. The factory boss said he could run up the jerseys in the short time demanded provided Desgrange was happy with yellow, an unpopular color and the only one left in sufficient quantity only a few months after the armistice. Either way it's a nice tale, and Eugène Christophe wore the world's first *maillot jaune* when he and the tiny bunch set off from Grenoble to Geneva on July 18, 1919.

But is even that true? Between the wars, there was a successful trucking business beside a main road into the Belgian capital of Brussels. It was run by Philippe Thys, a thoughtful man not given to boasting. Which is surprising because Thys had plenty to brag about. He won the Tour in 1913, 1914, and 1920, so if you remember that war meant no race from 1915 until 1919, Thys was in fact the first man to win three in a row. If he could be good enough to win a Tour de France only months after surviving the first world war, it doesn't take much to see he could have won a record five long before Anquetil, Merckx, Hinault, and Indurain.

It also means taking seriously anything he said. And what he said is that he'd been awarded a yellow jersey long before Christophe. When he was 67, he told the magazine *Champions et Vedettes* in Belgium that he'd been race leader in 1913 when Desgrange asked him to wear a colored jersey. Thys declined, saying he was already the focus of other riders' attentions and making himself more visible would do him no favors.

He said, "He then made his argument from another direction. Several stages later, it was my team manager at Peugeot, the unforgettable Baugé, who urged me to give in. The yellow jersey would be an advertisement for the company and, that being the argument, I was obliged to concede. So a yellow jersey was bought in the first shop we came to. It was just the right size, although we had to cut a slightly larger hole for my head to go through."

He spoke too of the next year's race, when "I won the first stage and was beaten by a tire by Bossus in the second. On the following stage, the *maillot jaune* passed to Georget after a crash." Now, these aren't flimsy memories or the kind of thing you'd make up. The detail is too convincing — and what would Thys have gained from inventing it 40 years later? Perhaps it was an experiment, a short-lived idea all but forgotten when it was revived six years later. We will never know. The Tour calls Thys "a valorous rider... well-known for his intelligence" and says his claim "seems free from all suspicion." But it adds: "No newspaper mentions a yellow jersey before the war. Being at a loss for witnesses, we can't solve this enigma."

The *maillot jaune* has a magical quality. It's been copied in color or principle across the world, from the *amarillo* of the Tour of Spain to weekend competitions for also-rans. The Giro has pink, the Tour de l'Avenir had a yellow jersey with two white stripes. It can transform a rider or damn him. It means chasing every attack. Rivals wait for the leader's *domestiques* to do the work, knowing they must. Having your leader in yellow is no blessing, especially early on. Winners have refused it if the holder lost it through bad luck. Merckx ignored it for a day in 1971 after Luis Ocaña fell on the col de Mente; Holland's Joop Zoetemelk rode without it one day in 1980 when tendinitis crippled Bernard Hinault. Nobody wore it the morning after a drunken mob knocked down Gino Bartali and flashed a knife in his face on the first day in the Pyrénées in 1950. Kübler inherited it two days later.

Jacques Goddet added "HD" to the left breast to honour the man whom even Tour archivists have called "magnificently mad." They remained until 1983, when they gave way to commercial logos. When I asked Goddet how he felt about it, he shrugged as only Frenchmen can.

Of all the jerseys in the Tour, the newest is the polkadot of top climber. Its design is also the least popular, although it stands out in the bunch better than either the green or yellow, especially since so many teams have adopted a referential patch of yellow in their own designs. Here, a supermarket chain celebrates its sponsorship with an effigy of Richard Virenque.

"You feel sad?" I suggested. A shrug, after all, could mean anything.

"Yes," he said, "I feel sad. But then times change and views change. We live in the present, not in the past." A diplomat.

The *maillot jaune* changed little for decades, unless you count the appearance and disappearance of floppy collars and front pockets. There was just one size, a deflated balloon on puny climbers or stretched across a sprinter. It was unbecoming to the dignity of the world's greatest race. It wouldn't seem a great expense to make different sizes. The Tour would still need only one a day. But Paris never hit on the idea or it dismissed it. Instead it turned the jersey into a straitjacket, the back slit and offered from the front. The winner pushed in his arms and assistants tugged the rest over his shoulders and fastened it at the back. It was kind on weary shoulders but it lacked the romance of a winner crowning himself.

The mountains prize began in 1933 but got its red polkadots only in 1975. They went to the Belgian Lucien van Impe, who won his first Tour next year. He won the mountains six times, more than he would, it was said, had his wife not nagged him to spend more time racing and less on his budgerigars. Only he (1971, 1972, 1975, 1977, 1981, and 1983) and Bahamontes (1954, 1958, 1959, 1962, 1963, and 1964) have won it six times.

The Spanish made wonderful climbers but rarely winners. Not until Bahamontes in 1959 did Spain win the Tour. He made the most of a French team fraught with friction, led through the mountains in dangerous weather (Luxembourg's Charly Gaul collapsed in the heat of the Pyrénées, only for the race to run into the cold and rain that he loved in the Alps), secured his lead by winning a time trial up the Puy-de-Dôme west of Clermont Ferrand, and rode into Paris as the winner.

Federico Martin Alejandra Bahamontes was nothing without hills. A heart-rending picture from 1960 shows him boarding a train back to Toledo after just three flat days. His was an era when riders had just ten gears and opened huge gaps. Inside rings on their Campagnolo chainsets went no lower than the 40s and riders pushed far higher gears up the climbs than now. According to Pierre Chany, they climbed incomparably better than modern mountain kings, although archive film of the mid-1950s and earlier suggest that tackling the mountains even for riders like Fausto Coppi was an exercise in survival and strength rather than sleek speed. But then again, the roads were bad and strewn with stones and holes even into the 1970s.

"You always have to watch out for climbers on the drops and in strong crosswinds," says Stephen Roche. Bahamontes had disliked descents since he careered into a cactus as an amateur. He once stopped on a mountain top in the Tour and ate an ice cream while the rest caught him. Better that than go down alone. His career ended in 1965 where it was made, in the Pyrénées. Baha, now old for a Tourman, trailed as Felice Gimondi took the yellow jersey and Raymond Poulidor moved into secure second place. He climbed off, pulled on his dark blue Margnat-Paloma tracksuit and joined startled lesser-lights in the back of the *voiture balai*.

Few riders impress in the mountains. Most resign themselves to grovelling bunches long in the rear. They call it "the Bus" in French —

The veteran French journalist Pierre Chany argued until his death that riders in the 1950s and 1960s climbed incomparably better than modern riders. What's more, he said, they fought epic battles over the toughest climbs, and to be first over the Galibier, the highest peak of the Alps, or the Tourmalet, its equivalent in the Pyrénées was a huge honor. Now the bunch bowls over some climbs without stirring, at speed but without drama. To those who seek to copy, however, as on the lonely reaches of the upper Tourmalet, the spirit of Charly Gaul and Federico Bahamontes lives on in the private battle of the soul.

l'autobus — in Italian it's *grupetto*. They chug fast enough to please the judges, slow enough to survive. The Dane Brian Holm said, "You get to the mountain and everyone gets in the *grupetto*. Everyone knows who they're used to riding with. Eventually you panic because of the time limit and the group can explode. You help each other out, but you don't make friends there. You give each other things like food and water, but only because you expect to get something back. A guy may be suffering, but you might need him later if you want someone to help you ride on a flat piece between the mountains."

Holland's Jelle Nijdam said, "You try to ride the flat a bit hard so that you can go up the mountains fairly slowly, then take the descents fast so that you can make up a little time."

Men on motorcycles ride up and down with blackboards, chalking the numbers of the breakaway and the time gap. The arrival of the chalk man alarms the autobus. It means it's dangerously close to elimination. Panic starts and it splinters. Those cast to their fate are later

Once they feared the bears; now the big climbs are an everyday challenge to les cyclo-sportifs. Tourist offices stamp the passage of those riding a circuit of cols and place signs warning them of the gradients ahead.

heard of on the list of eliminés in the press room. You get thrown out if you finish more than 15 or 20 percent slower than the winner. There are rare exceptions, such as Brian Robinson in the 1950s, whose hero-ism got him (but not his colleague Shay Elliott) back in the race next day.

The faster the stage, the greater the leeway. It could run from five percent for slower than 34 km/h to 12 percent for 46 km/h or more on flat stages. Rolling stages could run from six percent for less than 31 km/h to 13 percent for 37 km/h. The range in the mountains is more generous: from six percent for less than 26 km/h to 16 percent for 35 km/h. There are similar limits for time-trials.

A bit of science and a lot of emotion goes into classifying moun-tains. It's not simply the length and steepness but where they come in the race and the quality of the surface. The 300 m col de Borderes in the Pyrénées has been third category at the beginning of a stage but first category near the end. The north side of the col de la Madéleine varies from first category to *hors categorie*, the toughest, according to the day. The Alpe d'Huez climbs 1,200 m, relatively short, but it's *hors categorie* because the stage ends there, and at nine percent it's a leg-breaker.

The Alpe's eight miles and 21 numbered hairpins have been in the Tour since 1952, when Coppi topped it first. Dutch fans camp there for days among the estimated half-million spectators and Dutch riders try to win for them. Hennie Kuiper started the trend, and regular win-ners have included Joop Zoetemelk and Gert-Jan Theunisse. In 1992 the American Andy Hampsten climbed at record speed for the best win of his life and then in 1998 Marco Pantani trimmed his time even more. To put that ride into perspective, it took the American Lance Armstrong — the race leader — four and a half minutes longer to do it the following year.

The Tourmalet became a legend when Christophe broke his forks. But it spelled agony too for Belgium's Lucien Buysse, who took 17 hours in a freezing storm for the 326 km from Bayonne to Luchon, in-cluding the Tourmalet. Nearly 30 hadn't finished by midnight.

One day you should ride up the Izoard to the south side near the summit, the Casse Desert. Rock spires push from the bleak landscape. The Italian border is close by, and the Izoard has made memorable stages of the Giro as well. Close to the top are plaques celebrating men most associated with this Franco-Italian epic: Fausto Coppi and

Louison Bobet. The Izoard joined in 1922, crested for the first time by Jean Alavoine, hardly a chick at 34. Coppi and Bartali struggled over five passes in 1949 before Coppi could ride alone there to victory. Bobet snubbed the world on the Izoard in 1953 and 1954, and Hinault used the five-mountain route that Coppi had taken in 1949 to win in 1982.

The most unlikely climb is the Puy-de-Dôme. It's unusual because its two and a half miles are a dead end on a private road. You pay a toll to get to the top and, once you're there, there's nothing to do but ride back. Many detest the Puy, simply because it is so short and steep. There's no time to settle in, to work on a rival's weakness. Victory goes to whoever cracks last. It joined the Tour in 1952, along with the Alpe d'Huez and the climb to Sestriere in Italy. Coppi won all three. The Puy's most epic battles, though, came in 1964 and 1971. Poulidor and Anquetil fought wheel to wheel, Poulidor winning in the final kilometer, but Anquetil taking the Tour. And in 1971 Luis Ocaña crushed Eddy Merckx — only to crash in the Pyrénées. But both tales take more telling later.

11
Caravan Crossing

DESGRANGE hated bike factories. He fought them for 30 years, certain they took the sportsmanship from his race. By the late 1920s he was sure riders were motivated more by money than glory. His preferred distribution was glory to the riders, money to *L'Auto*. It helped confirm cyclists as the smallest big earners in the sporting world. In 1930 he scrapped trade teams and ruled that riders would from then on compete for their country. He was sick of the star system, he was tired of sponsors like Alcyon, which could buy the best riders, and of teams that operated as combines and not loose associations. Spectators could cheer not only their favorites but their country.

"Why [just] five national teams?" he wrote. "Because only five countries are in a position to provide a team: Belgium, Italy, Spain, Germany, and France. Luxembourg has only one man. Switzerland has only three. Austria just one. The other countries have none at all." The system kept out some good riders, among them Nicolas Frantz of Luxembourg, and Desgrange used his influence to keep out others, letting Belgium know that he didn't want to see Maurice De Waele, a personal dislike. In fact what happened was that the touriste-routiers now also had to be put into teams, which opened the way not only to French regional representations but teams of mixed nationality as well, which let Britons, Australians, and others into the Tour.

Perhaps Desgrange didn't spot the gap in his logic — he was ending team racing by introducing team racing. Maybe he was more worried by cost. If factories weren't to pay then he would have to. He had to pay for riders' hotels, their food and equipment. *L'Auto* was doing well but not that well. And so he hit on charging the stage towns and on opening the Tour to advertising. The caravan let in non-cycling companies. They paid, they advertised, and they gave away samples. Most popular was the Menier chocolates firm, which had for some time followed the race only to find many spectators had gone home. Now, in an official parade, it could go in front instead. Before long, the procession took longer to pass than the race, its highlight a motor-cycle acrobatic team, which legend said were off-duty Parisian police-men.

Now it's longer still but less exciting: 150 cars and trucks flinging razors, hats, maps, empty plastic bags, leaflets that nobody wants, and red metal badges indicating awareness of *le sida* (Aids). GAN, an insurance company, reckoned in 1994 to have gone through 170,000 hats, 80,000 badges, 60,000 plastic bags, and 535,000 copies of its eight-page newspaper. They weighed 32 tonnes. Coca-Cola's staff of 40 gave away 600,000 miniature cans of Coke and Minute Maid in 1998.

Desgrange hated team sponsors and eventually banned them and all their illicit tactics. For years the Tour was for national rather than commercial teams. Then the French cycle industry began to collapse and argued that it would disappear for good if Desgrange continued to deny them their one big advertising stunt of the year. No factories, no sponsors, no riders, no Tour, they argued. Desgrange crumbled and before long teams were sponsored by companies far larger than bike firms — reaching new depths, some argued, when a French money-lending company printed its phone number on riders jerseys.

Most largesse-flingers are students. John Graat of *Eindhovens Dagblad* wrote:

"Most don't care a thing about sport," says Angélique of Maison du Café, a trademark of Douwe Egberts. "I see the Tour as a way of earning money and traveling round with a great group of people and having a laugh." The earnings vary from company to company. At Lustucru Eggs they earn about 3,000 guilders [roughly $1,500]; at Maison du Café it's tighter at 1,000 guilders after tax. Most of the students are recruited through employment agencies. The most important requirement: to look a bit "representative." For AGF, an insurance company, it was extremely essential. AGF tries to attract potential policy-holders through 12 tight-faced lasses — blue shirt, white skirt — who ride on sturdy, off-road motorbikes. Every hundred meters they all have to stand on the pedals together. Their teeth may stay bared permanently.

"We have to stay smiling. I'm afraid I won't be able to get my face back to normal after Sunday," says one of the AGF girls after the finish in Morzine. The girls in the PMU cars are also on automatic pilot as they wave to the public. It's their duty. Even in this peloton the Tour starts to take its toll. By Paris they will have waved at 12 million people.

"I can enjoy seeing all those people," says Renée, a medical student in Paris. "But it's very tiring. I give out 10,000 binoculars a day."

Each vehicle costs around $10,000 to book its space and not a single one passes the finish without being welcomed with enthusiastic commercial plugs by the veteran *speaker*, Daniel Mangeas.

The caravan is disquieted when the Tour goes abroad, especially somewhere that doesn't speak French. Most stayed home when the race went to Britain in 1974, and French sponsors were curiously quiet even when it returned for two days 20 years later. That 1974 stage was a disaster. The idea — commercialism dictating sport — was to publicize artichokes and the ferry from Roscoff that exported them. Britain wasn't ready for the Tour, nor the riders for Britain. They disliked the long crossing, British Customs disliked teams bringing so many bikes, and Jacques Goddet forgot his passport and was said to have been kept under police surveillance all day. Fewer spectators turned up than expected and the riders did no more than pedal sullenly to a bunch sprint. Next morning the *Daily Mirror* asked: TOUR DE FRANCE: CAN 40 MILLION FRENCHMEN BE WRONG?

The caravan alerted commerce to the cheapness of cycling. The first extra-sportif was Nivea, a face-cream company, which bought a patch on Fiorenzo Magni's jersey. Others laughed — not least because the bald and ugly Magni wasn't the first man you'd associate with beauty cream. Nivea was joined by Chlorodont, a toothpaste maker, and then by a brand of Chianti. By 2000 everybody down to the supplier of shoelaces was getting a mention.

It was Raphaël Géminiani who introduced big-time sponsorship, selling cycling to the St.-Raphaël apéritif firm in the mid-1950s. Many were upset at sport selling itself to commerce. Tour officials were against because it would bring larger forces into the race and because advertising on jerseys was advertising that St.-Raphaël no longer needed to buy in *L'Équipe*. Magni, of course, was on Géminiani's side.

There was talk of strikes and protests, and an ingenious claim that the "Raphaël" on jerseys referred not to the company but Géminiani. The row enveloped the UCI, the international authority, and lasted until Milan–San Remo, the first time the new colors would appear. But compromise looked possible: the UCI was against outside sponsor-

For years Desgrange wouldn't even allow other newspapers on his race, let alone other sponsors. But choosing national teams cost him the support of the bike factories that employed the riders, and Desgrange had to find outside money to pay for his dream. Over the years, barely an inch of flat surface has been left unsold to advertisers... right down to the road itself.

ship, but its president, Achille Joinard, was in favor. According to Géminiani, Joinard told him: "Go to the start with an ordinary jersey. Just before the off, take off the jersey and wear your St.-Raphaël shirt. I will send a telegram forbidding you from starting if you represent an extra-sportif, but I'll take care that this telegram arrives only after the race has started." Why would Joinard undermine his own association? Because he saw *le sponsoring* as the future, and also, perhaps, because he was happy to push a stick into the Tour's wheel. The race, remember, had seen itself as bigger than the sport since it was criticized in 1904.

At first support was cautious. Cycling was unproven and there was no television coverage to show the advertising. The first support came from odd corners, including a night-club dancer called Myriam De Kova, the widow of a Greek who'd made a fortune in New York. De Kova was at least 70 but keen to become a bigger name. A Parisian cabaret owner called Jean-Marie Rivière introduced her to Géminiani, and De Kova was taken with the romance of racing. She employed riders in pink jerseys to advertise, in effect, her own legs.

In Italy, where extra-sportifs started, a sponsor stung by criticism that he cared more about money than sport began a second team with no advertising at all. It could have been a stunt — everybody knew which company it represented — but it shows even cycling has those uncomfortable with the influence of business. And it took a while to come to terms with it. The first outside sponsors were called not teams but "sporting groups," and the names of companies like Ignis (a refrigerator maker) and Carpano (vermouth) were preceded by the letters "G.S."

For a while sponsorship was a backer from outside the trade, like Ford or the Spanish lemonade maker Kas, then in smaller letters a bike maker like Gitane, and finally a supplier of widgets, such as Campagnolo. But since the 1970s the trade has had little more than a name on the frame. Sponsors have been strange: a Belgian soap company, a French moneylender, a Dutch maker of potato chips, a Catholic radio station. Drinks companies were shown the door when France became concerned with alcoholism. Cigarette companies were next. Unable to be a cigarette team in France, Boule d'Or of Belgium tried to associate itself with a French chocolate maker of the same name.

L'Auto at first banned other papers from following its race, then realized its mistake and allowed 15 press cars in 1922, five for *L'Auto*. Radio joined in 1929, when Jean Antoine, the boss of *L'Intransigeant*, and his colleague Alex Virot attempted a primitive outside broadcast on short-wave for Radio Cité. Broadcasting had barely begun when their car got blocked in as the riders sped off. Virot filled the time drawing caricatures while Antoine described the distant riders and the sound of Paris morning bird song.

In 1932 they set off again, now having arranged with the French post office to provide telephone land lines, which it hadn't until then considered part of its job. In a Jeep and a kitted-out truck they provided mobile coverage to a nation that listened agog. This, remember, was a nation still without paid holidays and frequently with a six-day working week. The sound of the Tour passing over the Aubisque on July 12, 1932, must have been the sensation of the year. The pair recorded the riders' passing, then went down the mountain to broadcast it an hour later.

Television followed in 1952, putting film on a train to Paris to be broadcast at noon the next day. The first live TV was on the Aubisque on July 8, 1958, followed by the Puy-de-Dôme in 1959. The big step came with a helicopter in 1960, which meant the Peyresourde and the Izoard could also be shown. Daily reports of the last kilometers started in 1962. The modern entourage has more than 1,000 journalists, generally the worst-dressed people on the race.

Radio and TV coverage of the biggest stages starts in France before the pedals turn and ends more than an hour after the finish. Behind the microphones are Patrick Chêne (left), who broke the Delgado doping scandal, and former winner Bernard Thévenet.

Up to 20 million, a third of the French population, are supposed to stand by the roadside to see, not an unfolding drama like a football match, but a whirl of color and chrome. They recognize barely a few. They are like citizens of other days, called to see kings pass in splendor without knowing why, without caring where. It is sufficient to have been there, to return with a silly hat.

Pierre Ballester, a reporter for *L'Equipe*, says the very roads become the property of the Tour. "It's the owner of the road for three hours," he says, "under the law. That shows the importance of the Tour de France." It's theirs until the broom wagon passes. For years, the *voiture balai* really did have a broom on top. Then, in 1992, the bosses decided brooms went out with Cinders. I'm told, though I've never looked, that tradition lingers: there is still a broom under the seats.

The *balai* drives behind everyone except the last police car but only minnows climb inside. Big-hitters call for cars or wait at feeding stations. A motorcyclist carries their number back to officials. The rest have only to touch the *balai* and their name will be on Radio Tour before they've taken their seats.

A hundred million are claimed for TV across the world, third largest after the summer Olympics. The contract is with France 2, the state channel, which combines with France 3 for sports coverage. Patrick Chêne and the former winner Bernard Thévenet work from a two-storey block of temporary studios, taking the slot closest to the finish. They commentate on the last three hours, and sometimes all day, on the mountain stages. They're introduced in shirts and ties, Chêne holding his microphone, Thévenet under a headset. Thévenet watches the same picture as viewers, Chêne has his screen split in four.

"I see less well than the average viewer, but I can see the pictures from the motorbikes and the helicopter as well as the view that people are getting at home," he says.

The motorbikes are manned by Jean-Paul Ollivier and Jean-René Godart, whom Chêne calls "the only true witnesses of the race." Every so often, when Ollivier calls in, there's a "Oui, Jean-Paul?" It's always a cheery "Oui, Jean-Paul..."

"I can't see Miguel Indurain," I heard him yell once as the leaders ploughed through the mountains. "Get the cameras back, get them back!" And moments later we saw what only Ollivier had seen, the one-time favorite dropped like an also-ran. Ollivier is the authority on history, both of the Tour and the countryside. Barely a chateau passes in a quiet spell without his being able to recite its history.

In the old days journalists rode on motorbikes in vest and shorts, notepads and wine in hand. No longer. Ollivier and the photographers still ride motorbikes, but reporters see little more than TV viewers, whatever their reports suggest. They sit in halls, compiling their "eye-witness" reports from the pictures, the race radio, the handouts, a few guesses, and some interviews.

Riders ascend the rostrum to Elgar-like music and step off into the clutches of France 2-3's Vélo Club, a television programed presented from an open-sided studio further along the finish straight. Once they stuck to the banal: "It was a hard day. I am pleased for my team-mates that I have won. I think I will be well placed in Paris. I dedicate this victory to my parents, my wife, and my darling daughter." Now they can often be far more lucid, providing television and radio with a breakdown of the stage that leaves newspaper reporters with a problem of what to write.

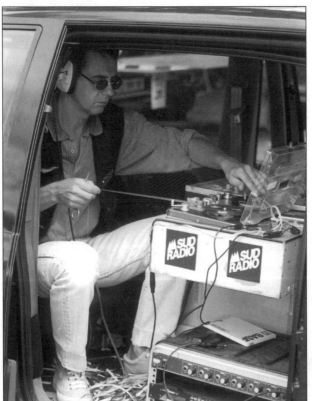

Radio stations break into their programs for Tour updates, and news bulletins regularly lead with Tour news. An army of broadcasters follows the race, chasing riders, collecting interviews, editing tape in cramped vans, and dispatching the result to the transmitters. Sud Radio is a station across southern France.

86

In the old days, too, they were willing to speak from their hotel rooms. The archives are full of riders lying on their beds with blackened arms, heads and legs and startlingly white bodies, chatting to whoever dropped by. Jean-Paul Brouchon of the news-radio station France-Info, said, "When I started, we called on riders without saying we were coming. You just had to knock on their door. Jean-Pierre Danguillaume regularly came into my room to cadge a cigarette. In 1970, I went to interview Rik van Looy after he abandoned. He was spread out on his bed, a cigarette between his lips. We all stayed in the town centers and the stages finished much earlier. In the evening, going for dinner, you could see them out for a walk in plain clothes, and you exchanged a few words. They didn't have all these public relations men and trainers and managers who isolate them today. I could even talk to them during the race, although that's been forbidden by the UCI now. Now relations are different. Laurent Jalabert doesn't give his telephone number, and he makes a point of changing it regularly so that he's not disturbed. Merckx, on the other hand, you could speak to any time you liked, and if he wasn't available then his wife Claudine answered." Riders like Jalabert, he says, don't respect the obligations of their profession.

Sometimes this intimacy hid things that ought to have been reported. It's never good for a journalist to become too close to the people he reports, for fear of confusing his allegiances. On the other hand, most specialist reporters are also enthusiasts and, while they may not be star-struck, they have often been keen enough on preserving a sport they love to leave out the odd fact or neglect the occasional question. As René de Latour said after Fausto Coppi had begun opening his heart about doping in Italian amateur racing, there was always a time when reporters felt happier putting down their notebooks. That's why, to this day, cycling and the Tour become alarmed and even angry when non-specialists concerned only with news descend on a race and begin reporting it with, as insiders see it, insufficient respect.

Discretion can amount to secrecy if a reporter tries to dig, and riders will be careful not to comment where a remark could backfire. The 1980s climber Robert Millar said, "It's a little world where you have to learn the rules. It's a normal thing anywhere you work. If you haven't learned the rules, you shouldn't say anything. If you violate the rules, no one likes you. If you annoy the riders it gets communicated between directors and you can be out of a job. They'll take the guy who fits in, even if he is on a lower level." Millar was famously taciturn, even abrupt, and his tact didn't always extend to reporters: "Guys see the race on TV, then ask you what's happened; you see them sleeping during the day because they've been drunk the night before. If I think they're useless, I tell them so."

In 1999, the French rider Christophe Bassons was one of a handful known to be riding the Tour without EPO. He had a newspaper column in which he chronicled his progress and then suggested that it was impossible to win a stage without drugs. The words were less frank, but that didn't impress his fellow riders and especially the stage winners and the maillot jaune, Lance Armstrong. Bassons was made an outcast, even within his own team, and he cracked and packed his bags and went home.

Cycling can sometimes be cruel.

Desgrange's annoyance with factories was so great that he insisted competitors use anonymous yellow bikes. That hadn't been the plan,

The broadcasters' technical area is a masterpiece of organization, with cables and transmitters and editing rooms arranged in strict pecking order — French TV right on the line, British and American TV relegated to small vans on the outskirts. In the middle of it all, overweight engineers more interested in signal strengths than leg strengths sit and drink beer and help themselves to salad.

but sponsors were so angry at being banned that they withdrew their bikes as well. Desgrange went to a "secret" supplier and got his own. When word got out who this secret supplier was — helped no doubt by the secret supplier — the sponsors were in a fix. They'd withdrawn their support but one of their stars would win on some rival's machine. Next year they allowed their bikes to be used once more.

National teams lasted longer than yellow bikes, but riders who spent all year as rivals weren't likely to co-operate just because they had a national jersey in the Tour. Their wages still came from sponsors. A Belgian might ease off when a team-mate riding for France should have been chased. Or a Dutchman might find it helpful to pace an Italian. There were more plots than the main story.

By the 1950s internal rivalry split not only teams but, worse for the Tour, French teams in particular. Some refused to take part if others also rode. Managers had to draw up peace treaties and before long French sponsors formed the Association Française des Constructeurs et Associés Sportifs to change the Tour's mind. They argued that bike factories were clanging shut as cars and motorbikes stole their market. Take their biggest publicity and there would be no more sponsors and no more Tour.

In 1962 the race went back to trade teams.

12
The Glory Years

FOR Jean-Paul Ollivier, "the best years were the Fifties. Cycle racing was not only at its peak, but it was rich with personalities. After the war, Europe was looking for its own personality. Cycling provided that. That's what the sponsors and the teams have all but killed off. The riders, the teams, are all the same.

"In the Fifties and to an extent the Sixties, it was a *phénomène*. The riders could say, 'I'm going to do it this way, my way.' And then, because Europe was moving again, there was a rivalry between nations — a good rivalry: France, Belgium, Spain, Italy, they all had their champions. Cycling carried those nations' dreams. Now, it's as if they come off a production line."

Ollivier began reporting races in 1961, starting with Coppi and watching Anquetil, Merckx, Hinault and Indurain win five Tours each. He doesn't expect a rider to win six. Careers aren't long enough. He's an affable, easy-going, grey-haired man who looks 50 but is a few years older. He sits in grey slacks and a pale blue shirt to one side of a table sprinkled with papers, up stairs beyond the glass security doors in the haute couture district of the avenue Montaigne in Paris. Models and millionaires mingle outside. The shelves include his own books about Roger Rivière, Louison Bobet, Jean Robic, Gino Bartali, and others.

He tells me, without looking, all the British team in 1955 — "Bedwell, Steel, Mitchell, Kreps, Maitland, Wood, Hoar — who finished last..." He gets as far as Brian Robinson and, feeling the need to keep up, I throw in that Robinson won stages. Ollivier tells me where and in which years. His role is to put glories and failures in perspective, and when things are quiet to speak of the battles or gastronomy of the region. He's forgotten almost nothing. We talked of Simpson's death in 1967 and he listed the team. He was annoyed at missing one name.

"It was Michael Wright," I said, not because I knew all the others but because I'd noticed Wright hadn't been among them.

"Ah yes," he said, "the Englishman who couldn't speak English." Wright had moved to Belgium as an infant from a backwoods town called Bishops Stortford. He spoke little more than 'hallo' and 'goodbye,' but always wore a Union Jack on his jersey and held a British racing licence.

"I was born in Concarneau, in Finistère. They grow up with the bicycle there. It's produced Hinault, Robic, Bobet. And so I've always loved cycling. I used to race a bit, and then I started writing about my hobby. I started following the Tour much later. That didn't happen until 1965, but I'd been writing about cycling since 1961. Then I was offered a job as political correspondent in Africa. That meant an end to cycling, but we always come back to our first love, don't we? I

Louison Bobet was a giant of the 1950s and France's largest magazine gave him the cover when he won in 1954. But his self-confidence let him down and his ambitions to become "un gentleman" made rivals laugh behind his back. He retired to run a sea-treatment company and a private airline which existed largely so that he could fly from one base to another.

made my first spoken reports on the radio on the day of my 20th birthday, May 22, 1964.

The Fifties were when they raced with collars, front pockets fastened by buttons, metal bidons stoppered with cork. Like Hugo Koblet, they wrapped goggles round their arm. More, though, the Fifties were poor in communication. Travel was for the wealthy, television unusual, and live TV sport rare.

The Fifties loved the fabulous, and cyclists were stars with a human dimension. Coppi had been an errand boy, Bobet a trainee baker. Anquetil was a metal worker and the son of a strawberry farmer. Crowds stood in raincoats and waited to marvel. There was, frankly, little else to do. And not only Ollivier pines. Francesco Moser, who beat Merckx's hour record, said, "Real champions don't exist any more. Once the teams were built around one rider. Now everyone rides for himself. Racing's more individual and it's harder for a given team leader to win. Back in the days of Bartali and Coppi, only the team leader counted. When I began, there were real domestiques in teams. When I stopped, they didn't exist any more.

"Domestiques pushed their leaders up the climbs and helped them with equipment, but that doesn't exist any more. In the time of Coppi, the domestique became important because he put you in the right place at the right time, so the leader could make a difference at the right moment. Then there was a hierarchy, but it's gone, and because the sport is so fast everybody can stay on the wheels longer. It's hard to make a difference.

"The fans are traditionalists who want to see races like they were in the old times. It's not possible now because the whole scene has changed."

The Tour halted for the war and began again in 1947, a waving invalid determined to show life still lingered. It left Paris on June 25, its 95 starters a mixture of old lags and newcomers. France wanted a lag — René Vietto. Instead it got a 25-year-old regional, Jean Robic, who ignored the convention that the yellow jersey is never attacked on the last day and put in a devastating ride on the Bon-Secours, one of the ring of hills surrounding Rouen, and won the Tour.

Robic was tiny, as a surprising number have been; Romain Maes, who wore yellow from start to end in 1935, was also tiny. Robic rode a 19-inch frame, but for a short man he turned unusually long 172mm cranks. He could push 44×21 where others rode 44×24. The French loved his courage. They liked the idea that a skinny lad with wing-nut ears should have made his name despite a bike too large and a habit of wearing soccer shorts. Journalists in Paris called him *le farfadet de la lande bretonne* — the goblin of the Brittany bogs. But many disliked him — especially the other riders — for being stubborn and spiteful. They laughed because he was tiny and ugly, like so many gifted climbers. Fans called him *Biquet*, which means "kid" or "sonny," enemies *tête de cuir* (leather head) for the sausage-like helmet he wore because he crashed so often. He looked as if he'd been through a few too many boxing bouts.

The big loser on the day that Robic took the Tour was Pierre Brambilla, a man with a big chin and a lot of confusion whether he was Italian or French. The surname was Italian and so was his family. But Pierre is a French name and he grew up in Annecy. The French had been quick to accept Maurice Garin in 1903 even though he'd been born in Italy but now the war was clear in memories, and devastation and signs of occupation still visible. More, Brambilla was riding

Nobody knows what Fausto Coppi would have achieved had his career not been spoiled by war. To many he is still the greatest, the most audacious. But he rode on too long, becoming a parody of himself according to Pierre Chany. He scandalized Italy but when he died the country came to a halt and his obituary ran to page after page.

for a team of Italians living in France. The bunch disliked Robic but it disliked "Italians" even more, and it did little to check Robic when he out-jumped Brambilla on the hill and got up to an innocent break. Briek Schotte won the stage but Robic won the Tour. Brambilla stayed bitter about this "betrayal" all his life, and legend says he buried his bike in his garden in despair. As for Robic, his personality, language, and behavior won few friends, and in the end they rebounded: two days before Paris in 1959 he finished outside the time limit at Chalon-sur-Saône and was eliminated, even though the bunch had done little more than amble at 20 mph. Any other former winner would have been reprieved.

Eventually Europe's enemies became simply rivals, the atmosphere that Ollivier loved. Teams and leaders appeared, the peak of the system which, say men like Ollivier, produced two dozen potential winners at every race — and a team to back them — rather than the six or seven of today. The greatest among them in that post-war era was a gaunt, heron-like man called Fausto Coppi.

Coppi, astrologers will tell you, was born on September 15, 1919, at 9:30 p.m. at Castellania in Italy, longitude 0°51′00″ east, latitude 38°01′ north. From that, presumably, they could forecast he'd be the first man to win the Tour and the Giro in the same year. You can find Castellania if you look at the top of the boot of Italy and find the port of Genoa. Now trace the main road almost north towards Milan. You'll see the road swing left to bypass a town still served by the old highway. That's Tortona, where Coppi ran errands for a butcher after World War One. Fifteen miles away is Castellania, Coppi's village. The road in which he lived is now the Via Fausto Coppi. Climb to the church and in the graveyard you'll find four copper poles about three feet high that list his biggest successes.

1940 Giro d'Italia

1942 Italian road championship; world hour record (not broken until 1956)

1946 Grand Prix des Nations; Milan–San Remo; Tour of Lombardy

1947 Giro d'Italia; Grand Prix des Nations; Italian road championship; Tour of Lombardy; world pursuit championship

1948 Milan-San Remo; Tour of Lombardy

1949 Giro d'Italia; Desgrange-Colombo Challenge; Italian road championship; Milan–San Remo; Tour de France; Tour of Lombardy; world pursuit
championship

1950 Flèche Wallonne; Paris–Roubaix

1952 Giro d'Italia; Tour de France

1953 Giro d'Italia; world road championship

1954 Tour of Lombardy

1955 Italian road championship

He overawed even those who worked for him. A photograph shows
him holding his bike in the Giro, a wheel lying on the ground. A mechanic is forcing a back wheel into the front forks. The caption says:
"Give me a revolver so I can shoot this fool."

Coppi raced professionally from 1940 to 1959, with a break as a
British prisoner of war in Tunisia in 1943. He was held until 1946,
when he won Milan–San Remo after four years without racing. His
chest was deep but not wide, his calves like an invalid's. He rode
humpbacked and narrow-shouldered. And yet there was odd beauty.
The French journalist Albert Baker d'Isy wrote that he had the "pure
lines of the Greek Acropolis combined with the streamlined fuselage
of a modern airplane."

André Leducq said, "He seems to caress rather than grip the handlebars, while his torso appears permanently fixed by screws to the
saddle. His long legs extend to the pedals with the joints of a gazelle.
At the end of each pedal stroke his ankles flex gracefully, a movement
that would be wonderful to analyze in slow motion on a cinema
screen — all the moving parts turn in oil. His long face appears like
the blade of a knife as he climbs without apparent effort, like a great
artist painting a water color."

I watched Coppi once, not live but on a film called *Of Sport and
Men*. He's on a long climb, two dozen riders in national jerseys strung
on his wheel. He looks half-starved, hollow-cheeked, ill. Nobody else
had the flopping, oily hair, the mouth that never quite fitted his face,
the globular eyes. He's on his small ring, pedaling quickly but not
fast. One mittened hand is on the bars as the other empties a cloth
bag strung over his shoulder. It looks like prunes. Only when he's
sure the bag is empty does he throw it away for a boy in short pants to
retrieve as a souvenir. Now he can get on with business. He places his

second hand alongside the first, rows harder on the bars and rides away from everyone else. Pierre Chany said, "it is a proven fact that between 1946 and 1954 Fausto Coppi was never caught once he had escaped from the peloton."

Coppi's greatest rival rode like an angel and looked like a boxer. Coppi and Gino Bartali crossed paths on January 7, 1940, when Bartali sat at Eberrardo Pavesi's house in Milan and put up with the old man's pipe smoke. Bartali called him Father, and Father was telling him whom he'd signed to support him in the Legnano team in the Giro. Bartali frowned. Coppi was too weak.

Weak? Bartali would see. Coppi stayed with Bartali after a crash on the first day and then survived by his side when attacks put the rest of the team out of touch. And this from a domestique. For the moment Bartali stayed leader. Then Coppi chased and passed a break on the Abetone and won by four minutes, even though Bartali had organized the whole Legnano team in chase. He became race leader and Bartali never forgave him. Their rivalry lasted close on 20 years. Italy split between the religious "peasant" and Coppi the slicker. Bartali ate with a religious statuette on his table and visited Lourdes. Coppi hid his atheism but never crossed himself before races. It sounds trivial now but the climate then was very different.

"I think the good Lord has better to do than worry about the gear ratios of bicycles," he said.

The more urbane Coppi appeared, the more his supporters loved him, but the more numerous became Bartali's own followers. Géminiani remembered: "During one Giro, when Bartali was the Italian national champion and very popular, the crowds would see his green, white, and red jersey and start chanting ! 'Gi-no! Gi-no!' This got on Fausto's nerves after a while, especially because Bartali had been riding very cautiously and exploiting the strength of our Bianchi team. One of our team-mates was a hulk of a man by the name of Donato Piazza, who was also the Italian pursuit champion. Fausto asked him to wear his champion's jersey and ride at the front of the bunch. The fans yelled and applauded, thinking it was Bartali. When the real Bartali went by later on, no one noticed, and Fausto was happy to pay the fines that Piazza got for wearing a jersey he was supposed to wear only on the track."

In 1948, Bartali won two days running at Lourdes and Toulouse and then every stage in the Alps — Briançon, Aix-les-Bains, and

Lausanne — and won in Paris. Next year the balance shifted. Coppi caught Bartali on the Izoard, and Bartali realized his career was over. He shouted for a deal: "It's my birthday. Let's finish together. Tomorrow you'll win the Tour." Coppi agreed: Bartali won in Briançon but Coppi took the Tour. He was so far ahead — he reached Paris with a record 28 minutes and 27 seconds — that Jacques Goddet had to double the money for second place. Riders were in such awe that a minnow called Jacques Vivier told reporters: "I thank Mr. Coppi that he allowed me to win this stage in front of my own people. Mr. Coppi is a gentleman."

Sadly, Coppi was plagued by crashes, broken bones and mechanical mishaps. He also made a huge misjudgment: he left his wife Bruna. *La Stampa* spotted him with a companion in a white raincoat and ran a picture with the headline *La Dama in bianco di Fausto Coppi* — Fausto Coppi's woman in white. The nickname added to the shame of adultery in 1950s Italy. Giulia Occhinni, like Coppi already married, was harassed by the offended husband, the public, the press

Coppi's bust stands outside the Madonna del Ghisallo chapel on a col near Milan. The little church, with its permanent prime line for the Tour of Lombardy, was dedicated to cyclists by the Vatican. Coppi's bike and yellow Tour and pink Giro jerseys are on display inside, along with those of many other riders.

and even the police. Detectives raided their house to see if she and Coppi were sharing a bed. Even the Pope asked Coppi to go back to his wife and, when he wouldn't, refused to bless the Giro while Coppi remained in it.

Sadly, he didn't know when to stop. Chany says that in 1959 Coppi was first to be dropped in the Tour of Spain, not just one day but every day. Promoters of criteriums cut their races to 45 km to be sure he would finish. Some blamed the Woman in White for expensive tastes, but Coppi didn't lack money. The tax office calculated he earned $80,000 in 1955 and 1956, that he owned estates and farms, a razorblade factory, and interests in two bike firms. They said Carpano was paying him $25,000 and that he was getting $800 for a track appearance even past his peak. They were colossal sums given that $20 a week would have been an excellent salary. His estate was worth around $1,500,000.

The worse he got, the more doped and broken he became. Chany called him "a magnificent and grotesque washout, a weary and disillusioned man, ironical towards himself; nothing except the warmth of simple friendship can penetrate his melancholia." He died aged 40 at 8.45 a.m. on January 2, 1960. He had malaria, caught on a safari in the Porga game reserve in Burkina Faso after some exhibition races with Anquetil and Géminiani in that country's capital, Ouagadougou. Géminiani, who also had malaria, survived with different treatment. Questions were asked in parliament.

A priest gave Coppi the last rites only after the Woman in White agreed to send him back to his family if he survived. The obituary ran forever in *Gazetta dello Sport* and for two pages in *L'Équipe*, where Goddet wrote: "It had been cruelly expected… We would like to have cried out to him: 'Stop!' And as nobody dared to, destiny took care of it." A paralytic walked to the funeral to say goodbye and traced his recovery to the day that Coppi gave him 10,000 lire. Anquetil, Bartali, Bobet, and Rivière were among thousands of mourners. The wreaths stretched 300 yards. The Woman in White sat with Faustino, their son, welcomed thanks to her repentance.

The coffin was carried by racing colleagues and preceded by a giant portrait. It was buried in earth brought from the Izoard. In one of many books about his life, a director of *Gazetta dello Sport* writes: "I pray that the good God will one day soon send us another Coppi."

13

The Summer of '64

COPPI AND BARTALI gave way to Raymond Poulidor and Jacques Anquetil.

Anquetil was languid and rarely attacked. He couldn't even name many of the riders in the bunch. But he lost nothing when it mattered and gained where it did — in time-trials, where he showered past everybody. He perfected the aerodynamic egg shape, low on the top tube, toes down, body shedding sweat. He rode like a man expecting a low bridge.

The name is Norse-Germanic. *Ans* was a title taken by war lords of the Goths, *ketell* means cauldron. Anquetil was never French professional champion, and certainly never the world's. In the classics, you'll find his name against only Liège–Bastogne–Liège. He was French amateur champion at 18, won a bronze in the team time-trial at the Helsinki Olympics, and then at 19 — not yet a full professional — he won the Grand Prix des Nations, the unofficial world time-trial championship, in Paris.

He was the most visible of riders but never sought or warmed to his public. He gave autographs awkwardly. He was admired rather than liked. He contrived with other French riders to let Bahamontes win the Tour in 1959 rather than their colleague Henry Anglade, who could have hurt their contract fees. The crowd shrieked disaffection, and Anquetil, with dark humor, bought a small boat and called it The Whistles of '59.

All this doesn't mean he lacks biographers. I had lunch with one of them, Richard Yates, in an unpretentious restaurant in Thouars in

99

central France. As his dog lay by our feet, tied by passing his leash round the leg of the table, Yates told me, "I still don't know whether I like him or dislike him or even if I really know him. There were several Anquetils. There was one Anquetil with the other riders, who loved him. There was the Anquetil at home by himself, and there was the Anquetil who knew the value of bluff."

I asked for an example.

"Look," he said, "when Anquetil won the Grand Prix des Nations, he was an unknown outside France. He went to see Coppi, who was the big star. In all the pictures you see of Anquetil in normal life, he's very smartly dressed, a man who likes, and can afford, clothes. But when he goes to see Coppi, he puts on peasant farmers' clothes to give Coppi the impression that he's just a country hick and that Coppi's got nothing to worry about.

"And he plays the peasant again for his press pictures after the Nations. This is a man who's never been a farmer, who went to a city college. And yet the pictures he arranged or at least contrived in after the Nations show him feeding corn to chickens and wearing clogs. Not on his farm but his father's farm. Anquetil? In clogs? And yet again, here was a man happy to deal with the press, whose voice is strong and clear and his opinions firm when he talks on television, and yet there are so many witnessed cases of his being too shy to go into a crowded restaurant for fear of being recognized that there's no doubt they're true."

A British wood merchant called Vic Jenner wanted Anquetil to ride a 50-mile time-trial between London and the Thamesmouth resort of Southend, then the fastest and most popular course in the country. At a lunch near London's Leicester Square, Tom Simpson told him time-trailing was the major part of British cycling and that courses were flat. *Cycling*'s editor, Alan Gayfer, asked Anquetil how long he'd take. Gayfer recalled, "Bear in mind he had no idea what the British record was. He said 46 minutes. The record was 54:23, to Bas Breedon. With no guidance, he estimated eight minutes off the competition record."

What made up for the cold brain behind the high-cheeked, well-coiffeured face was Anquetil's reputation as a playboy. A boy who asked how to prepare for a race got the answer, "With a good woman and a bottle of champagne." The journalist Jock Wadley once sat in his 12-bedroom chateau at Neuville-Chant d'Oisel near Rouen and played cards with him late into the night before a race. Anquetil loved poker but he often lost — because as in bike racing, his instinct was to risk too little.

Pictures at the height of his career show him dangling a cigarette, sitting in the sun in the gardens of Valleys Radio, downing beef and sangria, and living the life of the rich man that he was. They're from Andorra, a tiny state of 181 square miles in the Pyrénées, ruled since the 13th century by France and Spain in turn, and famous for skiing, tax-free shops, and a grasping attitude to tourists. Anquetil was enjoying the rest day of the 1964 Tour — and it all but cost him the race.

The start of the tale is that *L'Équipe* turned now and then to a clairvoyant called Marcel Belline, who'd predicted, "You will abandon because of an accident on the 14th stage." And sure enough, Anquetil rode like a stuffed pig. Antonin Magne, the strangely formal manager of Poulidor's Mercier team, (he addressed riders as "vous" rather than the informal "tu") had heard of Anquetil's self-indulgence and told Poulidor to play havoc with him on the col d'Envalira.

Anquetil watched the Tour ride away inside Poulidor's lilac jersey. His manager, Raphaël Géminiani, was desperate. He sent a tall, dark-

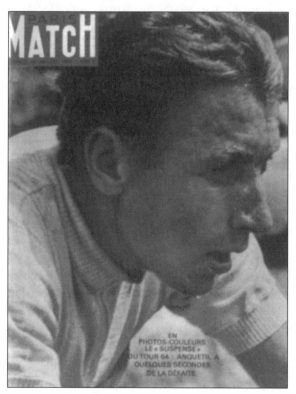

No rider has been as smooth as Jacques Anquetil. His shoulders moved so little that a glass placed on them wouldn t spill. He rarely rose out of the saddle and he was dropped as rarely as he dropped anyone else. He was brilliant but aloof and rarely knew the names of all his competitors. He remains an enigma to the French, who feel grateful for his victories but wish they had gone to Raymond Poulidor instead.

hared rider called Louis Rostollan to cosset him, appeal to his pride. "Have you forgotten your name is Anquetil?", Rostollan chided. But still he wallowed. Rostollan pushed him, keeping him going but losing four minutes. And then Géminiani looked ironically at the champagne he was keeping for victory and the solution dawned.

"It'll kill or cure you," he shouted, pushing over a filled bidon. Anquetil struggled on through low cloud, slowly coming round. He got back to the team cars and then, in a moment accorded only to the gifted, began descending the mountain as a pilot lands through fog. Blinded by spray and mist, he saw nothing but brake lights. Hairpins were invisible but not the lights as drivers pushed their pedals. Where they braked, Anquetil braked also, living on reflexes. He took horrible risks. And he lived.

He halved Poulidor's lead by the valley, then caught a group led by little Georges Groussard of the Pelforth beer team. Anquetil rode for aperitif maker St.-Raphaël, perhaps enough to rule out cooperation. But Groussard was also maillot jaune and he would lose without Anquetil's help. Both had reasons not to see Poulidor in yellow and together they caught the leaders. If ever Poulidor was unlucky, this was the day. Anquetil was back from the dead, Groussard had caught him, and now Poulidor flatted. Was that enough? No. Stage fright hit the mechanic and he threw the bike from the car so hard that it bounced and bloodied Poulidor's nose. Anquetil won a record fifth Tour.

By 20, Anquetil had been national champion, an Olympic bronze medalist, and won the Grand Prix des Nations. Poulidor at the same age had never even ridden in a train. That happened for the first time only when he was called up for the army. He still lives in Saint-Léonard-de-Noblat, near Limoges, where he grew up and won his first race. He laughs: "Yes, I know my reputation as a country boy. When I won a race, the other riders would say *"Tiens, Poulidor va s'acheter une vache"* — Poulidor can buy himself a cow.

He could make dreadful mistakes; a French friend told me he had *les jambes d'un cheval mais la tête d'une vache* — the legs of a horse but the head of a cow. In that Tour of 1964, when he came so close to winning, he raised his arm a lap too early on the vélodrome at Monte Carlo and threw away a minute's bonus that would have dislodged Anquetil. Anquetil made a pitch for the line and Poulidor was left to hurl his bike to the ground in fury. He stood on the rostrum year after year, but never as winner. Like the crocodile that ate Captain Hook's arm, he could do no more than follow Anquetil in the hope of tasting more.

Of Anquetil, he says: "I still think of him, not every day, but still from time to time. For a long time I detested him. We never ate at the same table at the post-Tour criteriums, and often it was his wife Jeanine who passed messages between us. With time, though, we became reconciled, and when he died I felt as if I'd lost a brother."

France was split between them just as Italy had divided between Bartali and Coppi. The figures varied but one year's poll showed 53 percent for Poulidor — mainly rural France — and 47 for Anquetil. Poulidor, who still follows the Tour as PR man for Maison du Café, can't explain why he had the edge, why even now crowds chant *Poupou* the moment they spot him. He never did like the name but he's come to terms with it. As a youth he was always "Pouli," but Poupou (it means "doll") stuck from the moment that Émile Besson of *L'Humanité* coined it in 1956. It lent itself to headlines like

The village of Quincampoix stands to the north of Rouen, and Jacques Anquetil set out from there every day to study engineering at the college in the suburb of Sotteville. He joined the cycling club in Sotteville and was coached by André Boucher. Francis Pélissier took him into the La Perle team and entered him for the Grand Prix des Nations, then the virtual world time-trial championship, at 19. Anquetil won... again and again. His marble grave is to the right as you enter the churchyard.

"Poupoularité," a play on "popularity," and satisfied a French instinct to shorten long words.

"Maybe it was my name that helped," Poulidor told Philippe Brunel of *L'Équipe* in 1999. "I had an easygoing smile, whereas Jacques had to force it a little. And then I had misfortunes; when I left the Tour in 1968 after a motorbike knocked me down on the road to Albi, I received 2,800 letters a day for two weeks. It was just as well they often had stamps for a reply or it would have cost me a fortune. In criteriums, I was alongside Jan Janssen, who'd win the race, but I was presented as the moral winner. Anquetil was irritated by my popularity. In some criteriums, organizers used to do me under-the-table deals so that Jacques wouldn't know I'd been paid more than him."

For many the greatest moment of their rivalry and the Tour itself came on July 12, 1964, on the Puy-de-Dôme. Anquetil had a German teammate, Rudi Altig, a tall man with a crew cut who as an amateur became a celebrity by standing on his head between track races. His dream was to win a stage and the yellow jersey while the Tour was in Germany. On the fifth stage, he beat the Dutchmen Janssen and Nijdam from Metz to Freiburt to win the points jersey and take second overall. Next day he cleared off with Groussard and a little group that all worked together except for the Belgian Willy Derboven, who was protecting van de Kerckhove in the yellow jersey. The Belgian won the stage, annoying everyone because he'd done nothing all day, but Altig became *maillot jaune.*

Usually it suits a leader to have a lesser light in yellow so early. But Anquetil was furious. Altig had taken Groussard with him and Groussard was as strong in the mountains as Anquetil was weak. Worse, Anquetil hadn't recovered from winning the Giro 14 days earlier. Sure enough, Groussard took the yellow jersey on the first stage in the mountains and Anquetil was eighth, almost a minute behind.

Then came July 12 and the Puy-de-Dôme. Anquetil was back in yellow but Poulidor stood every chance of taking it from him. An estimated half-million turned out and the race they saw is shown time and again when television tells the history of the Tour. Few remember that the stage was won by Julio Jimenez ahead of Bahamontes; the real race was below them.

Poulidor was consistently better. Anquetil could beat him dependably only in a time-trial, the only time he could rely on beating anybody. But Anquetil was a professor, Poulidor only a graduate.

Anquetil rode with a head like a computer and assessed time differences and vulnerabilities in a flash. While history forgets Jimenez and Bahamontes, Anquetil didn't. One story says he bluffed as he struggled to hold Poulidor. Poulidor could hear Anquetil's breathing above the noise of the crowd and the TV motorbikes, and he knew he was close to breaking. Then he heard him mutter *"Merde!... the Spaniards will get the bonuses!"*

It tricked him. Anquetil was stronger than he thought, relaxed enough to worry about the finish. Poulidor faltered and let him alongside and into moral check. It was always Anquetil's mental power that impressed. The pair brushed elbows. Only at the final kilometer did Anquetil crack. Poulidor took 42 seconds in the last 800 m, but it wasn't enough. Anquetil crossed the line with glazed eyes, still in yellow by 14 seconds.

The Tour therefore depended on its last 27.5 km, a time-trial from Versailles to the Parc des Princes on Bastille Day, the French national holiday. Anquetil was last to start, Poulidor immediately ahead of

Gone but not forgotten — Quincampoix placed this memorial to its fallen star in a small flower bed beside the village traffic lights. The picture shows him in his yellow jersey. More sacrilegiously, the one on his grave advertises Ford-France.

him. The crowd of 800,000 cheered Poulidor but mixed encourage-
ment with derision for Anquetil. There were six seconds in Anquetil's
favor at midway. And then he reached to his unfashionable downtube
levers for his highest gear. He won by 21 seconds with another 20 in
bonus. Poulidor got nothing, not even second place. That went to
Altig, who'd started all the trouble back in Germany.

Poulidor never did win, but next year, and even in 1974, he came
second. He never even wore yellow. The closest he came was 0.8 seconds in the prologue of 1973. *L'éternal second*, the French called him.
Anquetil said, "He always comes second, usually behind me. And still
they shout more for him than for me. If he loses, he doesn't have to
find excuses. But if I come second or third, then I've failed. They'd
call me a calculator, a strategist, even though miscalculation had just
made me lose."

Poulidor said, "When he stopped racing, he became my greatest
supporter, because of his daughter Sophie. It seemed she could say
'Poupou' before she could say 'Papa.'"

I've never spoken more than a bonjour to Poulidor, but I did have
a faltering conversation with Anquetil. I was an apprentice at
Heathrow airport in London when a French colleague spotted a blue
Gitane on a trolley from the Paris plane, made a guess, and walked to
the transfer lounge to confirm it. Anquetil was sitting in jeans and a
leather jacket with a cup of coffee. He may not have welcomed a
teenager with schoolboy French, but he showed no sign. I saw him a
few times after that but it took another decade before I could mention
it. We met briefly at the Tour in Plymouth, he then ghostly and dying
of cancer.

"So it was you," he said, claiming to remember. It was just part of
the man's charm. He won in 1957 and every year from 1961 to 1964.
He won the Giro in 1960 and 1964 and the Tour of Spain in 1963. But
still France is unsure how it remembers him. He brought France more
Tours than any man before him and nobody has beaten his record
since. Equaled it, yes, and even won as many in succession. But
beaten it, no.

He was on the unfashionable side of the doping argument that he
did so much to start. He spoke for the right of cyclists to treat themselves with whatever they chose while that same right was open to
others. He saw no difference. Or, at least, he objected to the hypo-
crisy that allowed one man to make his work easier but not another.

He led a strike against dope tests in the Tour of 1966 and he was quietly dropped from the world championship and the next Tour as a result. He was denied the world hour record after refusing a dope test in a makeshift enclosure in the middle of the Vigorelli track in Rome. Champions and unknowns alike had a right to dignity, he said, and not be forced to pee behind a screen with 8,000 looking on.

Pierre Chany recalled, "Jacques had the strength — a strength for which he was always criticized — to say out loud what others would only whisper. So, when I asked him 'What have you taken?' he didn't drop his eyes before replying. He didn't lower them in front of me or in front of the others. He had strength of conviction." Others died from drugs or shot at lampposts. Anquetil behaved with dignity, once winning the Dauphiné-Libéré stage race and the 345-mile Bordeaux–Paris without a night's sleep between them. Chany said, "You can't be a champion like that just by taking a pill from a bottle."

Anquetil retired on December 27, 1969, bitter to the end that the French government had sent a telegram of congratulations to a Belgian, Ferdi Bracke, for bettering the distance that he, a Frenchman, had ridden in that hour on the Vigorelli in 1967. He spoke for drugs but declined surgery when he developed cancer in 1986, and he went on working until surgeons removed almost all his stomach. His wife Jeanine says Anquetil had a constant fear of dying. When his father died at 56, he became sure he would never make the same age. He didn't. He was born on June 8, 1934, in Mont-St. Aignan in the hills around Rouen, and he died on the morning of November 18, 1987, in the nearby clinic of St.-Hilaire. He was 53.

He lies now in the churchyard in the center of Quincampoix, the village north-east of Rouen where he lived as a boy. It stands on a minor road that runs almost rod-straight from the Rouen suburbs. You're in and out in moments. The village sign is just before the single set of traffic lights, alongside the Brasserie de Commerce, and the end-of-village sign — the name struck through with a diagonal line to mark the end of the 50 km/h limit — only a few pedal strokes later. If your eyes are on the *feux*, the traffic lights, you may miss the tall, black marble memorial on the right. It stands back in a small flower bed, its gently curved face showing Anquetil in his characteristic swept-hair, high-cheeked riding style, and lists his record.

The village is to the left. Ignore signs for the cemetery — that's round the back of the village, it's new and almost empty. Go instead to the entrance to the church, ironically next to a pharmacy — Anquetil's final link with this world as he was carried to the next. Turn right at the war memorial and you'll find Anquetil's grave in the middle of the second row.

It's black, shaped like a tall narrow book, with his signature picked out in gold on its open pages. There's a short tribute from fellow cyclists in the Sotteville club at his feet, and a picture etched in silver of him riding his bike. The memorial at the junction had him in an anonymous jersey; here on the grave, with an air of the sacrilegious, he has the advertising of Ford-France embroidered on him.

I began to focus my camera and became aware, as I had with Maurice Garin at Lens, of outside interest. A short man in a cap and a cotton jacket made his out-of-focus way across the top of the picture screen and then, seeing me, stopped. I took my picture and waved my thanks. He didn't need to stop but he'd shown consideration.

"Something of a hero," I called, by way of explanation. He came over.

"You're not the first," he said. "There are quite a few people over the year. I walk through here every day and I see them over there" — he pointed to more graves on the other side of the church — "and show them where they need to be."

"You knew him?" I asked.

"I knew him when he was a boy. One of my sons used to play with him. He lived just over there. But soon he was very rarely there, and eventually he bought his big house." I asked what sort of *mec* he was, what sort of a man. To us he was an enigma, I said. He made one of those ouff noises that only the French can make and said that was how everybody else saw him as well.

"And he...," he gestured putting things in his mouth..., "too much."

"It was normal for the times," I said, mistaking him.

"And not only champagne," said my man, oblivious to my misunderstanding, "but beer as well." And then, by way of a non-sequitur, "you know his brother is an insurance agent, do you?"

Insurance broking must seem gratifyingly simple compared to frère Jacques' life. His wife, Jeanine Boéda, had been married to his doctor. Anquetil decided from the day they married in 1958 that she was to live as a country lady. But peace she rarely saw. Anquetil not only struck up an affair, but an affair with her own daughter from her previous marriage. In 1971 he gave daughter Annie a daughter of her own, Sophie. He and Jeanine separated. And then in 1983 he had an affair with Dominique, who was the wife of Alain, who was himself the son of Jeanine. And Dominique too presented him with a child, Christopher, in May 1986. By those standards even Coppi's life seems straightforward. Jeanine lives now in a two-bedroom apartment in Paris and says nothing bad about her husband, from whom she divorced two months before his death.

Eight thousand said goodbye to Anquetil at Rouen cathedral. The Tour stopped to pay homage next year when it passed his grave. In 1983 Quincampoix's 2,000 residents named their sports center after him — it stands, cement-stained and unloved, to the left of the church beyond a wall that has a notice saying "Fix no notices to this wall." In 1997 the memorial service on the tenth anniversary of his death drew Miguel Indurain, Eddy Merckx, Bernard Hinault, Felice Gimondi, and Raymond Poulidor. Ironically, given Anquetil's mastery of time, the main guests got stuck in traffic and arrived late.

14

Ici On Parle Anglais

IN 1928 Walt Disney created Mickey Mouse and in the same year the first English-speaking team entered the Tour. One was deliberate comedy, the second accidentally so. Now, this was the first team. The first riders were the Australian isolés Don Kirkham and Ivor Munro, who finished 17th and 20th in 1914. The view that anglophones were urchins standing outside the party could have been encouraged by news that Britain had abandoned road racing in the 1800s after a pack of tricyclists near Cambridge upset a toff on a horse. As bad, but less eccentric, the USA had lost interest after being the best in the world. The U.S., remember, supplied the world sprint champion of 1893, 1898, 1899, 1904, and 1912. America had 600 professionals before 1900 and kids collected their pictures. Americans decided who was best and then went to Europe to sort out whoever was left. But then cycling died. Ford and fashion saw to that.

In continental Europe they'd seen the giants. There was something to copy, to aspire to. But racing in English-speaking countries became pay-at-the-gate or early-morning penance against the clock. The grit-in-shoes misery of British time-trailing was kept secret even within the sport. Cycling magazines couldn't say where a race was to be held, nor report it fully afterwards. Dates and courses were in code, race instructions headed "Private and Confidential." Competitors dressed in black and carried no numbers.

Small wonder that Britain was so short of talent that in 1933 it picked Percy Stallard for the world championship because he could run up a hill faster than the others. In the shop that he ran in

Wolverhampton in the English Midlands — it still had a box marked "Osgear spares" — he told me, "The test hill [the main hill on a circuit used for testing cars] that you had to go up five times was so steep that on the first lap I pulled my foot out and I ran up. I was in the lead then and several other riders passed me. I couldn't get back on my bike at that steep angle, so I ran past these other riders and won the prime at the top, running! And that happened for the next two times. I won three laps like that, running up the hill in a cycle race. It's farcical, really. But that's why they picked me." Stallard had no training kit and surveyed the Montlhèry circuit in khaki shorts and shirt. The Continentals called him "Boy Scout." It was only his second road race — the selection event was the first — and he came 11th despite crashing.

To the Tour, cycling in America, Britain, Australia, Canada, and New Zealand had died. The flickers it saw were just specters come to see what might have been. It's an irony that the breakthrough came from so far away. In 1927, the *Melbourne Herald* decided three Antipodeans should support Australia's long-distance specialist Hubert Opperman, plus six Continentals it'd find separately. Opperman was special: half English, half German, he could ride a horse bareback by six and plough with six horses. As a post office messenger, he rode an antiquated bike until 1 a.m. He was Australasian cycling champion by 1924.

Opperman and the others went to a training camp run by Paul Ruinart of the Vélo Club de Levallois near Paris. They rode Paris–Rennes, a 200-mile race that had André Leducq among the starters. He'd just won Paris–Roubaix. Nicolas Frantz of Luxembourg came first and Opperman finished eighth. Then Opperman came third to Frantz and the Belgian champion Georges Ronsse in a break of three in Paris–Brussels after the other two had worked him over for miles. Two months later the Tour started. Unfortunately the promised Continentals didn't turn up and 15 stages of the 1928 race were a team time-trial. One was 387 km long. And there were only four in the Australian team, remember, compared to the ten of all the others.

At a retirement retreat in Melbourne surrounded by "No cycling" signs, Opperman told Alan Gayfer, "They gave us three days [to prepare]. We were riding with the whole of Australia expecting us to win. Crikey, those team time-trials were hard. You couldn't feel your legs. They were like blocks of wood. The hardest race that I have ever ridden. We were riding the Pyrénées on dirt tracks in the middle of the night."

Even so, Australia finished third on one stage and Opperman was 18th in Paris. Harry Watson of New Zealand (described as looking more like a priest than a bike rider) was 28th, and Percy Osbourne of Australia 38th. Alcyon signed Opperman, and three weeks later he recovered enough to win race after race, teaching himself to pee on the move on a fixed wheel so he could win the Boule d'Or 24-hour on the Buffalo track. The French voted him their sporting hero, and a gendarme stopped the traffic in Montmartre to let him pass. A poll in Melbourne put him ahead of the legendary cricketer Don Bradman.

"If we didn't race, we didn't have money. So we always raced," he said. He came back to the Tour in 1931 but dysentery pushed him from sixth to 12th. Australia and its neighbors had tried and done well, but the Tour was still for the French and their neighbors. Australia forgot its debut, and the rest of the English-speaking world was not bothered. To find how unbothered, go into a Canadian newspaper office and look through back issues for 1937 for how much — or little — you find about Pierre Gachon riding that year's Tour. Even *Cycling* in Britain carried only a few paragraphs, and that despite two Britons riding for the first time.

In June 1937, Gachon and the Englishmen Bill Burl and Charles Holland rode the Tour for the Empire. That the Empire's 800 million realized they were riding is doubtful. And they didn't have long to catch on. Gachon was thrown out after losing his way between Paris and Lille on the first day, and Londoner Burl was eliminated after a crash on the way to Charleville. As well as the first Tour with derailleurs, this was also the first with service cars. Holland was demoted to last after following one up the Ballon d'Alsace. He survived for 15 days and 2,000 miles until the Pyrénées, and there he punctured, 30 meters behind the leaders on the col de Port, stranded like a novice. Today he'd have rejoined within the mile. But there was no radio and, at that moment, no service.

He tore the tire from the rim, replaced it with the spare knotted round his shoulders, and began pumping. The Empire's pumps weren't all they might have been, and Holland got to no more than half-pressure. Drivers showed no sympathy and so he climbed back and pedaled towards the top, looking for a spectator. A Frenchman obliged, Holland flatted again on the descent. He'd set off with the permitted two spares and now there was none.

At his home in Birmingham, England, opposite the newspaper shop bought from his earnings as a pro, he recalled: "A crowd of peasants had gathered around me, but they couldn't help me. A priest bought me a bottle of beer, and although it quenched my thirst it got me no further. After I had given up hope, a tourist came along and gave me a tubular touring tire. I put it on, and in the excitement the rod of the pump broke. We blew the tire hard with another pump but the tire fitted so loosely that it came off with the fingers and so was unsafe. Another tire was found that fitted a little better, and again I set off, but I had by then given up hope. When I arrived at the control, where we were to receive food and drink, the officials had gone."

Belgian journalists tried to persuade him to go on. But "I took my number off and definitely retired." He died at the end of 1989, when he was 81. Which meant he was 47 before Britain fielded a team of its own.

Retired now in the house among the hills of northern England where he lived at the time, Brian Robinson describes 1955 as "like racing cars competing against Concorde." Nevertheless, sponsored by the Hercules bicycle company, he became the first Briton to finish. He was 29th, and the only other survivor was Tony Hoar, who came last and found himself in demand all over France. The rest dropped so regularly that Robinson said he felt like one of 10 green bottles hanging on a wall. Three years later he won a stage. The race had gone 50 of 170 km when he went off with Arigo Padovan of Italy and the Frenchman Jean Dotto. Angels were more likely to fall from clouds than any of these three win the Tour, so while the race relaxed, Robinson got rid off Dotto but found himself stuck with Padovan into Brest.

"He hadn't a smell of winning," he remembers. "It was a long uphill finish and I put my head down and went." He was in 52×14, dropped to 16 and kept going. Twice Padovan pushed him into the crowd before finishing first, but the judges gave it to Robinson. In 1959 he won by 20 minutes, or seven miles. Padovan was again second. Many English speakers have won since, but none remotely close to that margin. Yet.

15
Look at Their Bikes

A LISTAIR SKINNER's bike is one shade darker than leaf-green. Hand-painted yellow lines run parallel down the main tubes. The Idéale leather saddle is broad and worn, the handlebars and front fork and rear stays bare metal, plated with nickel to a dull sheen.

"I can't say definitively that it was ridden in the first Tour de France, but it's been handed down the generations with that understanding and it's certainly of the era," he says. He bought it from an elderly Frenchman who'd grown tired of it. It's been in his house between Leicester and Loughborough in the English Midlands ever since.

"It's the forks that catch you out," he warned as I stepped on to it. "The rake is enormous, so the first thing that happens when you sit on it is that the wheel will turn sideways and the bike will swing round backwards." By modern standards the flat, semi-swept bars are impossibly close to the saddle. The pictures of old riders with arms vertical, cycling as if they were operating a stirrup pump, are not unfair. With narrower bars it would be impossible; in reality, you get used to it. It means you can get your nose down almost on to the front tire, and that's the way they streamlined themselves. If you give yourself a mile, you can really get it whipping along."

The bars must have been old-fashioned even then. They're the style that the American world champion Arthur Zimmerman used on the track in the 1890s. Dropped handlebars were already in use by the start of the century. The shallow forks are more maneuverable than you'd guess. There are no front drop-outs, though. Fitting the wheel

114

is a matter of forcing the forks apart and slotting the axle ends through the slots. The rear dropouts open backwards, track style, and there are untypical square cut-outs in their broad face presumably to save weight. It weighs perhaps 26 lb., half as much again as Pantani's best bike in 1998, but still light against James Moore's. The wheelbase is enormous.

"It's so long that I hang it on the rack that supports my other bikes and it touches the floor, whereas the others are well short." It measures 190 cm from tip to tail, 1m18 between the axles. Tires are tricky too. They're an eccentric 28 x $\frac{3}{8}$ inch.

"Michelin haven't made them for 60 years," he says. "I came across them in a bike shop in Belgium. The chap asked if I wanted anything else and I laughed and said 28 x $\frac{3}{8}$ inch tires. He went out the back and brought me a couple of dozen for 20 pence [30¢] each. They must have been there all those years."

I tried it. Not far, because this is a bike with no brakes. You stop by pushing back on the 75-inch gear and its inch-pitch chain. There are no drillings, no fittings for brakes. Nor is there a freewheel; that didn't

I was assured it was ridden in the 1903 Tour de France, says Alistair Skinner of the brakeless machine he keeps in his house in the English Midlands. The wheelbase is enormous and the fork rake so soft that it can catch you out. But that just made it better for the unmade roads of the era. At the turn of the century, remember, there were only 10 miles of surfaced road in the whole of the United States. France probably wasn't that different.

arrive in the Tour until 1907. The long wheel base would have been excellent on rocky roads. The broad saddle and its springs would help with stages that started before dawn. The pedals aren't original but they're still held by both thread and clamp bolts. The tubes are heavy, set in uncompromising lugs. The chain stays are a single wide tube as they leave the bottom bracket and then divide in a curve, like a modern integral fork crown. They look like the front forks of a mountain bike.

"Not typical," says Skinner, who collects bikes of all ages and has both a high-ordinary and a tandem recumbent in the same room. "I don't know why they did it." He thinks it's a Peugeot but, while the paintwork is old, it's not original. The replacement head badge, itself many decades old, says "Cycles Chavigny, Blois."

"I'd love to know who rode it, but it's impossible to know." It must have been someone tall for the age. The frame is 24 in., above average even today.

By 1905 the Tour had two categories of bikes: *poiçonnée* and *plombé*. *Poiçonnée* riders could mend their bike but change none of the parts. The stars preferred *plombé* and the right to change components. The hardship of a *poiçonnée* led to a category for riders who could finish on the same bicycle. Lucien Mazan, known as Petit-Breton, won it twice. And why is Lucien Mazan shown as Petit-Breton? Because his family thought cyclists were disreputable.

"To them, to ride a bicycle was to bring dishonor on the family name," he explained. "So the first time I raced, without their knowing of course, I was asked my name and of course I hesitated. I said 'Breton... I'm a Breton.'" But it turned out there was already someone else in the race called Breton, so because I was younger they entered me as Petit-Breton." He was also known as *l'Argentin*. Word says his father was a clock-maker, defeated devastatingly in his attempt to become a politician in 1890. Ashamed, he moved from France to Argentina, where Lucien got swept into bike racing.

A picture of how life could be in those days came from Vernon Blake in *Cycling* on September 23, 1920:

> The bugle sounds anew; Thys and Hector Heusghem sprint for second place. Mottia pushes Vandall against the hurdles to the right where both fall five yards from the line; Scieur, Masson and Lambot profit by the occa-

sion to pass them. Barthelmy passes me with a front wheel, snapped clean in half, strapped on his back, a borrowed one in the forks.

The Tour has been unusually hard. The almost universally execrable state of the roads united itself, till Perpignan, to continuous rain, which then suddenly changed to insupportable heat in the Alps. Then again, in the early morning on leaving Strasbourg the fields were covered with hoar frost. The men are loaded with three or four spares, food for four or five hours in a satchel, and a waterproof. On account of "summer time," 50 kilometers of each stage are ridden in the dark.

I noticed nothing particularly new in the matter of mechanical contrivances. The moyeau à broche, or hollow axle, seems to have definitely lost favor with French racing men. Almost all modern machines are fitted with the type of long back-ends opening forwards and slightly downwards which allows for a big difference between the two freewheels. Change gears other than the wheel-turning method were forbidden this year by the rules. Thys rode with 65 and 48 [-inch] gears; all the other men used approximately the same combination, the extreme limits being 70 and 44.

The derailleur was news to none of these men. The Frenchman Paul de Vivie, better known under his pen-name Vélocio, made a double crankset at the turn of the century and, while it worked, the rider had to pick up the chain with his fingers. Only touring cyclists could be bothered. Joanny Panel used a primitive derailleur to get over the Télégraphe, the Galibier, and the col d'Allos in 1911, but it was condemned as unreliable when he didn't finish the race.

Competitive cyclists preferred a fixed sprocket on one side of the hub and a freewheel on the other. Gears, says historian Ralph Hurne, "were for tearaways, tourists, softies and vicars — and definitely not for racing." Real racers jumped off, turned the wheel, pedaled up hills, freewheeled down, then switched to the higher fixed gear for the flat. At first there was just one freewheel sprocket, then a choice.

Roger Lapébie, first to win with a derailleur, recalled:

We had big fork ends at the back of the bike to make chain adjustment possible. In the mountains we used a 44-tooth ring at the front with a 22 and 24 on one side and 18 and 20 on the other. On the flat we had a 50-tooth ring at the front with 16, 17, 19 and 20 sprockets at the back. Flexibility and speed were important. You had to change the gear at the right moment. On the flat you would put it in the right gear, or you would go as far as you could up the hill, then change. You could lose a race if you didn't change gear at the right moment. If a good rider stopped to change gear, everybody might attack together and he would never see them again. There was a lot of psychology involved.

Men jumping off to turn their wheels appealed to Desgrange. He wanted man to master his bike, not to be helped by it. He insisted on tool kits, that riders finish with a much-mended bike rather than a replacement. He watched early gearing with a heavy heart and stood out against derailleurs until 1937. By then the battle was pointless. Riders had become adept at switching from one ring to another — although not always as adept as they'd like. As Peter Nye points out in *Hearts of Lions*: "It was not uncommon to see a veteran fixed-gear rider with a joint or two missing from the finger of the right hand, from getting the finger caught between the chain and front sprocket while tightening a toe strap."

Various people had a go at a decent derailleur. The hour-record holder Oscar Egg saw an early version in France and patented his own version in every country except France, where it was already protected. It made him a rich man. A guide hanging from the chain stay twitched the chain from one sprocket to the next. There was a sprung arm with a single sprocket behind the chain ring to take up the slack and, to modern eyes, it looked as though it was the gear itself. It was as clumsy as it appeared. Then, in 1928, the Frenchman Lucien Juy made the Simplex double-pivot derailleur. The mechanism moved from beneath the chainring to under the sprockets, where it is now. Two spring-loaded pivots could cope with five sprockets, although many preferred four. It wasn't perfect but it was better than what followed, and the modern era had started.

Juy's gears were good but he didn't have the commercial flare of an Italian racing cyclist called Tullio Campagnolo. Campagnolo was born in Vicenza on August 26, 1901, and his company history says he was "a rising star on the Italian cycling scene." Rising, perhaps, but nobody seems to have considered him a star, although he was on the team that won an Italian team championship and he finished the Tour of Lombardy, and Milan–San Remo. Legend says he abandoned a race across the Croce d'Aune pass on November 4, 1927, when snow numbed his fingers too much to change a wheel. A better engineer than a cyclist, he patented the quick-release wheel in February 1930, although it didn't catch on quickly; even in 1951 riders were still using butterfly nuts.

Campagnolo these days is in a white hangar by the Milan–Venice road. Then, he had only a workshop behind a hardware shop. His first gears weren't as good as Juy's, and they arrived to only mixed success on May 4, 1933. Rods and levers released the back wheel and let the chain stretch to the next sprocket. It meant pedaling backwards while moving the rods and levers that loosened the wheel, moved the chain, then tightened everything up again. If you pedaled forward before locking the wheel, it flopped forwards out of the frame, and the bike locked up. Gino Bartali could manage it without slowing but Fausto Coppi used it only because Campagnolo sponsored him, finishing the Grand Prix des Nations furious at "this complicated gadget."

The modern Campagnolo derailleur came in 1951, by which time the firm had grown to 123 employees. It had handlebar controls and a cable-operated front changer and it was far better. People stood and marveled, even though in brass it was heavy by today's standard.

Desgrange denied his riders service on the move, and competitors sometimes carried broken wheels for miles to justify to officials that they hadn't accepted a replacement without good reason. The ban was just Desgrange's stubbornness, because support cars had been known in cycling since the start. They may not have been as slick as we know them now but they were around, as this picture from a 1907 issue of **La Vie au Grand Air** proves.

Coppi had it and so did his two Bianchi team-mates in the national team; Bartali and two other Italians on Bartali bikes had it; and Switzerland's Hugo Koblet had one. The total — seven. A handful had cotterless cranksets, considered dangerously flimsy, and nearly all rode Simplex gears.

And why did Simplex and other French companies lose their grip? Gerald O'Donovan, who looked after race bikes for Raleigh in the 1970s, says, "The problem was getting the French to agree on a common set of parts. They just would not get their game together. I believe still today that the French component industry shot themselves in the foot by failing to co-operate with one another. They would have been in a much stronger position to resist oriental competition. But there, I am forgetting that M. Chauvin was French."

Desgrange surrendered to gears, but he still insisted riders replace their own tires and carry two spares, one beneath the saddle and the other round the shoulders. Many carried compressed-air cylinders as well as conventional pumps. Gears brought tactics and pushed up the speed enough for riders to shelter in bunches. There were two hours and 49 minutes between Maurice Garin and his runner-up in 1903. In 1998, the same margin covered all but one of the entire field.

16
The Emperor and the Cannibal

R IK VAN LOOY had forgotten I was coming. He'd told me to meet him at the Bloso, outside Herentals, near his home in the marvelously-named Poederlesesteenweg. Bloso is a health and sports center, and when you get there you see signs in the woods that say *Wielrenners!* The word means racing cyclists and it's unlikely that anywhere outside Belgium has signs warning of cyclists out training.

I rode past the signs and down to the single-storey Flemish Bike School, between tennis courts and an ice rink. It was shut. Venetian blinds covered the windows and the lights were out, but through glass doors I could make out a poster of van Looy climbing a hill in his Belgian champion's jersey and, close to it, a sign announcing "Doping? Not me!" Van Looy wasn't at the Flemish Bike School on August 22, 1970, either. He was in a Mercedes on the way back from Valkenswaard in Holland. He'd had enough.

"I was tired of riding against snot-noses who, even if you took them all together, hadn't managed a fraction of what I'd achieved," he told me when he found me on the doorstep. His eyes were as burning and his smile as Halloween shaped as when Belgium called him *Keizer*, or emperor. "And yet sometimes when they'd beaten me, I'd hear them say, 'Oh, we gave that old geezer a hard time today.' So, above all else, I stopped because of the break of respect. Physically, I could have gone on. The training was getting harder, but I could still do it. But I couldn't take that disrespect. They knew what I'd achieved and how difficult it was to do it. And these little riders thought they could laugh at me."

He won 500 races, including every classic — the first was Ghent–Wevelgem in 1956 — and two world championships, five stages of the Tour, six of the Giro, and 18 of the Tour of Spain. What he never won was the Tour itself. Look at the records and you'll see Belgium first won in 1912 and kept on winning until 1922. De Waele followed in 1929, Romain Maes in 1935, Sylvère Maes in 1936…, and then nobody.

Decades passed when Belgians rarely got on the podium. The country went into introspection, wondering why it could produce sprinters and one-day winners but not tour riders. It passed laws to encourage amateurs to turn professional early. But the result was not tour riders but specialists in the round-the-houses races that many saw as the death of "real" racing. And then came Eddy Merckx. The name is sufficient to link a nation split between languages. The improbable consonants identify it as Flemish, from the northern half that speaks cottonfields Dutch. The first name, though, is Walloon, pleasing the French speakers of the south. Had he been solely Flemish, he'd have shortened his name to its last syllable — Ward. Better, he came from the Woluwé-St.-Pierre suburb of Brussels, the largely French-speaking capital that is nevertheless an enclave in Dutch-speaking Flanders. So he was Eddy.

He arrived suddenly. He flatted in his first race, changed a tire, passed the bunch and won a prize. The judges said he'd taken a short cut. By 1964, he was world amateur champion, almost still a junior. His parents couldn't spare time from their grocer's shop to be with him in Sallanches, in eastern France. His mother is said to have asked for a sign she could see on TV if he was riding well. She suggested he freewheel on the last lap and shake his legs twice. Sure enough Eddy gave his legs two shakes. There was huge excitement, and half an hour later he stood on the podium above his team-mate Willy Planckaert and Gosta Petterson, one of a family of Swedes who promised much but disappointed. Momma Merckx placed a call to France. She thanked Eddy for that sign. Sign? What sign? He'd shaken his legs because they were tired.

Merckx turned professional next season, won nine races in his first year and 20 in his second, including Milan–San Remo. The French wanted him to ride the Tour in 1967, but Merckx and Peugeot, his French team, were cautious. He was young and Belgium had thrown too many hopes into the coals. He rode the Giro instead, came ninth and won two stages including one in the mountains. And then he became world champion again.

"Eddy moet de Ronde!" Belgium chorused — Merckx must ride the Tour. Merckx recalled the prime minister's telling him, "Don't let yourself be influenced by the pressure you're getting and you'll continue to be put under. Be sensible and don't get into something you don't feel is in your best interest." And then the killer hint: "Like other Belgians, I hope you take part in this Tour because you've got the best chance of taking the yellow jersey. But you are at liberty to make your own choice." Merckx wasn't just a bikie; he was important to crown and state. He stayed away.

By 1969 he was ready. He went to the Giro for training, built a huge margin over 19 stages — and was disqualified in a drug test. Eight times he'd been found negative. Belgium fumed about a plot. Merckx gave more samples, in the presence of journalists, and a lab in Milan cleared them. But the tests weren't official and the UCI banned him for a month, enough to rule out the Tour. Belgium appealed and the UCI suspended the sentence. But it didn't clear him. Merckx considered throwing it all in.

This was a fresh crisis. It was one thing if he decided not to ride the Tour, but to be prevented from riding it was different. A joke in Europe says you can't name ten famous Belgians. There's Georges Simenon, who wrote the Maigret detective stories, and Agatha Christie's Hercule Poirot, and the cartoon character Tintin — except the last two are fictional, of course. Belgium did, though, have a Formula One star in Jacky Ickx. And Ickx talked him round.

Lance Armstrong brought American interest back to the Tour in its closing race of the 20th century. Once, American money was seen as the future of cycling, and the dream eventually cost a Tour organizer his job. All the same, nearly a hundred years after the race started, the yellow jersey's sponsor still thought fit to take out an ad explaining how it's awarded.

Merckx attacked on the seventh day and drove the field off his wheel up the Ballon d'Alsace. He finished alone, took the yellow jersey and let nobody take it back. He pitched up on the Aubisque with almost seven minutes and said he'd just wanted to see who the opposition was. He won the Tour by 18 minutes, and a legend had begun. He had the yellow jersey, the points race, and the mountain competition. He held the white jersey as best placed in the other three. His Faema team won the team competition.

I was in Belgium that summer and came home with an Eddy Merckx tea-towel. I could have had Eddy Merckx chewing gum, keyrings, or T-shirts. He won five of the seven Tours he entered and spent 96 days in yellow, 18 more than Bernard Hinault. He won 34 stages, six more than Hinault. He won an average of a race a week for the next six years. In the midst of all this hysteria, a photographer sneaked into a changing room and published a poster of his naked backside; Merckx had to sue to have it removed.

This domination was real. The French champion Raymond Delisle said of the Midi-Libre in 1969: "When you know how much money Merckx has won in this race, you lose the will to try. At the same time, important firms interested in cycling hesitate to invest considerable sums in a team of professionals they know will inevitably be beaten."

I put that to Rini Wagtmans. This craggy Dutchman was Merckx's leading *knecht*, seeing off the king's rivals with his lance. He lives near Wim van Est, in St. Willebrord, where he runs a sportswear company. He still has the white patch in his hair that led the bunch to call him *Kuifje*, or Tufty. The idea that Merckx made the sport dull irritated him.

> He was a born athlete, and you can't say that was bad for the sport simply because he was the best. The domination was complete, but it happens in music as well as sport, doesn't it? Every ten years you get a dominant figure appearing, and that means the other guys have to pick up the crumbs. But there are always dominant figures. I mean, think of Elvis Presley, Michael Jackson, think of Mozart and Strauss, think of other people in sport — Carl Lewis. They're all people who are only born every ten years or so.
>
> Merckx won a lot, but it was never boring. We got a lot of pleasure from it. And having to ride for second place isn't good fun, of course, for the opposition. But when your team leader comes first, well, then you forget that." But then, if Merckx had such talent, what need for a team of

lesser lights behind him? What use does a boxer have of a sparring partner he could fell with the first blow?

It's easy to say that a super-champion doesn't need helpers. But he has to be sure that in the first 150 km of a Tour stage, if he gets a flat, or if suddenly there's a turn and an echelon starts up — and getting an echelon set up is really difficult — and then if Merckx has had a flat tire and he's in the second or third echelon, you've got to get him back to the first row. And then you have to be 100 percent behind him, which is incredibly difficult. But then, as a team man you can take the losses. But not the leader. He can't lose a minute or two minutes.

I reminded him of the *forçats de la route*, whom Albert Londres had described — the convicts, the laborers, the slaves of the road. That's how it sounded, breaking your back, bursting your thighs, biting the handlebar tape to close gaps for your master.

No one looked better in pictures than Merckx. But appearances can be deceptive. In reality, he rode like an animal, fighting his bike.

"No," he said. "I never felt like a slave. I mean, if a butler comes to your table and he asks politely what you would like and you tell him nicely, then he doesn't feel like a slave, does he? He is earning a crust for himself as well as for his family. And a pro rider, he's got a *knecht* — as you said, a road slave — but people do that to earn a wage for themselves."

It's hard to think that Merckx ever wavered. But he did. There were times, too, when he was close to having no sponsor. The Dutch clothing chain C & A once backed him for a year to bridge him between bigger concerns. And in 1975, wearing the rainbow jersey and having already won Milan–San Remo, the Tour of Flanders, and Liège–Bastogne–Liège, he cracked to Bernard Thévenet. Merckx was in yellow with two minutes' lead as he reached the mountains. He faked tiredness in the Alps and then attacked alone. Drivers couldn't keep up on the drop. Merckx had a minute with four miles to Pra-Loup but Thévenet came back even harder. Merckx cracked two and a half miles from the top and staggered to the finish. Thévenet took his yellow jersey next day.

"I tried everything and it didn't work," Merckx said. "Only the strongest can win. And Thévenet is the strongest."

Worse, though, was 1971. Nobody doubted Merckx was on his way to Tour five. He took the lead, Molteni won the team time-trial, and Merckx won the second stage. But Merckx faltered in a flurry of attacks on the Puy-de-Dôme and let Luis Ocaña get away. Ocaña was a good-looking Spaniard who'd given Merckx a hard time in the Dauphiné Libéré. Anquetil was on the radio urging him to get stuck in still harder. And so he belittled Merckx by nine minutes on the way from Grenoble to Orcières-Merlette. Merckx pleaded with the bunch that Ocaña was a danger to them all. But a man who'd inflicted misery on everyone, cut their earnings by reducing them to runners-up, wasn't about to be rescued when he was in danger himself.

Word spread that night that Merckx had been taking even closer interest in the way his mechanics prepared his bikes. He'd been down in the garage instead of eating and resting. Something was up. The crucial morning started black and dreadful, the Pyrénées shrouded in black. And far from improving, the rain turned to hail on the road from Revel to Luchon. Merckx was unmerciful. Ocaña had ridiculed him and now he was to be led on a roller-coaster of agony.

Again and again Merckx attacked, and repeatedly the Spaniard resisted.

Together they reached the col de Mente and started the descent. Now the weather became atrocious. The col is a long succession of curves and bends — the last place you want to be in bad weather. Two and a half miles down, Merckx missed a left-hand turn, skidded in running water and fell. Ocaña too came crashing down and ran into a low wall guarding the ravine. Merckx put his chain back, Ocaña got to his feet and took a wheel from his manager, Maurice De Muer…, and then Joop Zoetemelk, who ran straight into him, blinded by rain. He was followed by Joaquim Agostinho and Vicente Lopez-Carril. Ocaña took the blow in the kidneys and collapsed howling, his yellow jersey spattered with blood and mud.

Jacques Goddet stood in the mist looking spectral in a white waterproof, waving the followers to slow down. The race passed and left the Spaniard to the helicopter that took him to hospital at St.-Gaudens. Anquetil, whose urging had innocently contributed to events, visited him that evening. Merckx refused the yellow jersey and sat at Ocaña's bedside when the Tour passed his home in Brittany. Ocaña poured champagne and Merckx wished him luck in 1972. There's a plaque now on the right-hand side of the bend remembering the event. The Spaniard recovered and won the Grand Prix des Nations, and two years later the Tour itself. But his was a brief career. The question is still whether Merckx had met the only man to humble him or if Ocaña had been merely a biting flea.

Is it fair to illustrate Merckx's career by a rare failure rather than a list of successes? I think so. The exception tells the tale. After all, the man's superiority was such that in the 1971 Super Prestige Pernod, Merckx won more than twice the points of the second, third, fourth and fifth — combined. It was the occasional failure that made the news; victory was merely expected. There is no greater sign of a champion than that.

17
Counting the Beans

CENTRAL PARIS is surprisingly small. Something like one in four Frenchmen lives in or around Paris, but the *centre ville* is small enough to walk around. In the year the Tour first finished on the Champs Elysées, I walked to the Seine from where my train arrived and stopped for one of those high-octane black coffees that kick-start the republic each morning. A television showed the bunch riding gently, chatting and playing for the cameras. Real racing wouldn't start until the city.

When I looked back as I left, I noticed a dark blue plaque beneath the street name. It listed three, maybe four names. And below them the words "Shot dead here by the Germans in June 1943." It's only then that the impact of the war in an occupied land comes to you.

In 1914, Henri Desgrange was all for war, glory, and spilled blood. He wrote in red ink: "My lads! My dearest lads! My lads of France. Listen to me! In the 14 years that *L'Auto* has appeared every day, it has never given you bad advice. Well, listen to me! Believe me: it is not possible that a Frenchman succumbs before a German. It is a big match that you have to play: use all of your French skills... Go! Go without pity!... The Prussians are bastards. I don't use the word just to talk dirty but because it says exactly what I mean. When your bayonet is against their chest, they will beg for mercy. Don't give it to them. Drive it home without pity!"

The old man lived just long enough to see war break out again, but his last years weren't comfortable. He got the Tour as far as Charleville in 1936 and then reluctantly handed it over to *L'Auto*'s editor-in-chief, Jacques Goddet. Desgrange was 71, and he hadn't been well since surgery five years earlier. He died at his villa in Beauvallon on the Côte d'Azur on August 16, 1940, and there's now a memorial to him on the Télégraphe. By then the bloody enthusiasm of 1914 had been replaced by the reality of invasion, Germans on the streets, and men *fusillés* outside cafés. *L'Auto* carried on publishing. More, in the words of those who nailed its doors shut on liberation in 1944, it "submitted to German control" by printing Nazi information. Perhaps it had no choice. It's difficult to live those days if you weren't there.

With *L'Auto* gone, Goddet established *L'Équipe* on the other side of the road. On the first front page he wrote, "We are living through a cruel time in the life of a society in which, if we fail to resist it, selfishness will become the dominant passion. Against such a threat, we will fight in the name of solidarity. *Équipe* [team] — the very word exercises a noble influence on the heart of our group — an influence that was exerting itself during a time of rage and hope when our collective will was placed in the service of the Resistance."

Goddet became Tour director. I met him in the barren office that *L'Équipe* kept for him in the rue Rouget de Lisle in Issy-les-Moulineaux even though he was in his 90s. His name was on the door and there was furniture in the room, but no papers, no sign of work. His skin was leathery and he spoke difficult, gravelly French, but he was bright and active. I had to say his name three times to the receptionist before she remembered who he was.

"They called Desgrange the Father of Tour; I am Victor Goddet's son, so I became the Son of the Tour," he told me. Like Desgrange, he wrote from the front. He editorialized as much as informed. He too wrote in belle époque phrases to bugles and rolling drums, paragraphs that rumbled like tumbrels in a cobbled street. He spoke not of finish lines but *les arrivées magistrales*. He composed spiraling sentences about *géants de la route* and their *calvaire* and of Louison Bobet "accepting gallantly the delay attributed to him by the celestial handicapper." He had other of Desgrange's habits, reveling in the toughness of the race and rarely making himself invisible. He adopted colonial gear of khaki shorts and shirt, knee-length socks, and a pith helmet in the sun of the south, and peered through his car roof like a tank commander.

"It was just chance the first time I did it," he said, "but when it proved popular I did it every year. It was certainly cooler and it added color to the race."

I first met him in Holland in the 1970s. He reminded me of Charles De Gaulle. He carried himself with the down-the-nose haughtiness that explains why the French have a strutting cockerel for an emblem. I found the French to ask what the Tour cost to organize. He told me it was twelve and a half million francs. And then, as he stepped out of the elevator, he shook my hand and added: "Old francs, of course, monsieur." France hadn't used "old" francs for decades.

Goddet was educated in Britain — but only until he broke his arm at rugby and went back. He ran the Tour when English-speaking riders were a novelty and anglophone journalists from however minor a paper were "from *The Times*." His notorious press officer, Louis Lapeyre, refused to speak to them, let alone in English. He would deal with them only through Jock Wadley. Goddet now had an assistant, a commercial director. Félix Lévitan grew up in the 13th arrondissement of Paris, where his parents were shopkeepers. He became head of sport at *L'Équipe*'s sister paper, *Le Parisien Libéré*. Now it's just *Le Parisien* and a tasteless tabloid, but the full name — "the freed Parisian" — had a resonance for Lévitan because as a Jew he'd hidden from the Germans. Between them they turned Desgrange's race into a what it is today — buoyant but increasingly tarnished. The racing was fabulous, but the rest was commercialism and cheapness.

"And now," said cynics, "the coureur with the happiest smile." If that sounds ridiculous, remember cycling did have an award for the friendliest rider (*assuré* by the Outspan fruit company). The Communist *L'Humanité* sneered that everyone must have a prize and every prize a sponsor. Change looked essential and in 1981 it looked like coming. Lévitan spoke for half an hour as he unveiled the following year's Tour and ended with a statement so unexpected that he repeated it. There could be no Tour, he said, unless things stayed as they were. The press room was astonished. The Tour had become such a hurdy-gurdy that serious papers were suggesting the government itself should run it. It was part of the *patrimoine*, the heritage, and it needed protection from itself.

Well, the Tour is nothing if not capitalism. It would approach nationalization only with the sign of the cross. Lévitan stressed the Tour cost "not a centime" in taxes, that its $3 million paid for Paris–

Roubaix, the Tour de l'Avenir, Bordeaux–Paris, and other races that lost money. And why should the publicity caravan be any more outrageous than "soccer, rugby or motor-racing — especially motor-racing with its illegal advertising of tobacco and alcohol?" If companies paid $1 M for teams, were they not entitled to logos on the jerseys? That, after all, was all they got.

He said the Tour generated work for 70,000. It paid $400,000 to the police and for telecommunications, more than $600,000 in wages, $50,000 for staff expenses, and $250,000 for hotels and meals. And so it went on, down to filling the cars with gas. The Tour was safe, but the cost was more than 50 sponsors and 13 jerseys or awards after each stage. First prize was no longer a check but an apartment by the sea at Merlin-Plage, and only then some money. The apartments may have been worth the quoted 120,000 francs — the first prize in 1982, with 30,000 francs on top — but things are worth only what you'll pay. If you didn't want an apartment at Merlin-Plage, it wasn't worth much at all.

Pedro Delgado, Stephen Roche, Greg LeMond, Bernard Hinault, Laurent Fignon, Bernard Thévenet, and Lucien van Impe would all be neighbors if they'd taken them. Hinault won five and could have gone into the vacation business. By 1988 first prize had become a Peugeot 405, a Merlin apartment, 500,000 francs, and "a piece of art." Things were getting ridiculous.

Goddet and Lévitan dreamed of glory but kept the yard unswept. Goddet dreamed of *mondialisation*, a Tour that started in America, crossed Britain, and rode round the Continent before spending the last five days in France. Every fourth year, France, Belgium, Holland, Italy, Scandinavia, West Germany (with Austria and Luxembourg), Britain, and Switzerland would field professionals. The USA, Canada, Portugal, Poland, Colombia, the Soviet Union, Czechoslovakia, and a batch of African countries would do what they could with amateurs.

It never happened. But two things followed. First, cycling got its World Cup, a points race to spread cycling beyond its heartland. And

In its masthead, **L'Equippe** remembers its roots.

then in Cancale, in Brittany, in 1982 Lévitan opened the next year's race to amateurs. He wasn't bothered about Africans but he did throw in Bulgaria, Romania, and Venezuela. Unfortunately the only amateurs in the end were from Colombia, and they produced some superb climbers, like Luis Herrera, now a cattle breeder back home and amused to hear that so, too, is Bernard "Hinoll," as he pronounced Hinault. They were fun but the only lasting consequence was that years later Jean-Marie Leblanc saw unhappy South Americans waiting outside a call box to phone home and insisted that from then on all Tour hotel rooms had telephones.

For the Tour, desperation had overreached itself. Goddet was growing old and Lévitan wasn't much younger. Relations between them were said to be sour. Lévitan slowly took over and peaked when Émilion Amaury bought L'Équipe and the Tour in May 1965. He was an Amaury favorite. Fondness, though, didn't extend to the rest of the family, and Amaury's son Philippe gave him the push on the morning of March 17, 1987. Lévitan arrived to find the locks changed and a court official with a search warrant. His office was searched, cleared, and he was banned from Tour headquarters in a row about alleged cross-support of a race in America. Lévitan insisted he was blameless, went off to the Mediterranean at 76, and sulked that Amaury had cast doubt on his honesty. He told a lawyer, Jean-Jacques Bertrand, to look out for libels.

"We never see him at races and he'll never talk about cycling or the Tour. It's very sad," L'Équipe's Pierre Ballester told me in 1997. And then a year later Lévitan turned up grey-haired and in his eighties. The surprise of L'Équipe and everybody else was obvious. "The organization and I have come to respect each other," he said enigmatically.

Goddet became director-at-large before leaving a year after Lévitan. The new director, a cognac company manager called Jean-François Naquet-Radiguet, lasted a year before he went off to television, seemingly disillusioned with brakes on his ideas of progress. And then came Leblanc, an amateur saxophonist who rode his first race among unlicenced riders in 1961 and won his first real race at Bousies in May 1962.

In 1967 he became a professional even though he'd rather have been a journalist. He'd always wanted to for La Voix du Nord in Lille — in fact he rang the sports editor, Émile Parmentier, and asked and got a part-time job in the gap between being an amateur and the start of his professional contract.

"I know you," Parmentier said. "You're a local rider. You can start next week." Leblanc was amazed. It made such an impact on him that he still remembers the phone box he was standing in at the time. He moved from there to become chief cycling correspondent for *L'Équipe*. He'd studied law and economics. He'd also ridden the Tour, and that level of education made him an intellectual of the peloton.

He said, "My first preoccupation has been to restore the Tour's sporting credibility. We have simplified the Tour, which had become incomprehensible to the public, and cut the trophies from 12 to six, with just four classifications: the yellow jersey, the winner of the stage, the polkadot jersey for the best climber, and the green jersey for the points competition. These steps to magnify the athletic spectacle have already borne fruit. And sponsors have returned. Cutting the number of *partenaires* has increased their visibility, which means we can charge them higher prices."

He and Jean-Pierre Carenzo made sponsorship 56 percent of the budget, or 92 million francs. France TV agreed 50 million francs a year to keep the Tour until 1997. Television rights to more than 30 countries bring a further 50 million. The 30 stage towns pay an average 600,000 francs, and the start town 5.5 million. Teams no longer pay 300,000 francs to enter, and riders share more than 11 million in prizes — two million for the *maillot jaune*, 150,000 for the green jersey, 50,000 to stage winners, and 100,000 on mountain stages.

"We wanted to offer the sort of prizes offered in the greatest sports events in the world, like the Roland Garros tennis tournament [in Paris]," Leblanc said. The Tour now costs about $20 million, rather more than Goddet's "old" francs. The company also runs or has run the Critérium International, Paris–Roubaix, Liège–Bastogne–Liège, Paris–Tours, and the Grand Prix des Nations. It does, though, maintain a distance from *L'Équipe*. The bridge that joined newspaper and race offices has been removed, as symbolic as it is irritating to reporters who have to walk in the rain to get from one to the other.

It's a sign that the Tour has finally distanced itself, too, from the old days. From now on it's a business as much as a tradition.

18
Stars in Stripes

THE U.S. had more cycling talent than any other nation on earth at the end of the 19th century. Augustus, or Arthur, Zimmerman was the first world cycling champion and Major Taylor the world's first black champion, nearly a decade before Jack Johnson in boxing and 15 years before Joe Louis was even born. Both had their troubles. Zimmerman faced the awful fate of being banned by the British for posing in Raleigh advertisements but Taylor, born long before his time, faced repeated harassment and discrimination because of his color and died penniless in a charity ward in Chicago in 1932. He was buried in an unmarked grave in Mount Glenwood cemetery with few mourners before fellow cyclists moved him to a memorial garden there in May 1948.

Peter Nye quotes Victor Breyer, Desgrange's deputy who waited at the top of the mountain, as calling Zimmerman "the greatest pedaller of all time, regardless of nationality, speciality, or time." A French spectator "was moved to describe Zimmerman's style" in the heat of blasting for the finish "as if the man was mounted on rails, so complete is the absence of wobbling and the semblance of effort."

American pro racing plunged in the Depression. Bobby Walthour, its great promoter, lost his home and worked as a tram driver and school-crossing guard. America's wooden tracks had gone by the end of World War Two. An entrepreneur with the Mob-like name of Jimmy "The Whale" Proscia ran sixes in Chicago, Montreal, Cleveland, Buffalo, Toronto, and Minneapolis and they attracted riders like Hugo Koblet, the so-called "pedaller of charm," who won the Tour by 21 minutes in 1951. But six-day racing was more or less all the professional racing there was. And then it died.

The revival started with the women. As Soviet troops rolled into Czechoslovakia in 1969, Audrey McElmury became lone winner of the world road championship. She opened the way to Beth Heiden, Sheila Young, Sue Novara, Connie Carpenter, Rebecca Twigg, and Connie Paraskevin — all world champions on the road or the track. The veteran reporter Geoffrey Nicholson rates the performances but suggests women's racing was the underbelly of world racing, something only Russians took seriously and a few others succeeded at. But no matter. The point was that America, the forgotten land, was producing champions again. But why?

Cycling was never strong in English-speaking countries. But there was an important difference in the U.S. Not only the sport had died. So had the bicycle. It had become a toy, balloon-tired and shaped like the motorbike its owner was presumed to crave. Nobody cycled to work. In Britain, by contrast, people did still ride to work. That should have meant a cycling culture and eventually champions. But it didn't. Britain took to the car with the enthusiasm of Americans, and to an extent because of them. Stricken by rationing until long after the war, their luxury goods going abroad to restart a bankrupt economy, they looked on lasciviously as Hollywood showed America as a road-cruisin' paradise. The bicycle stood for the old world and class repression. Girls went out with boys with cars. Only failures rode bikes.

America didn't see the bike with the same prejudice, so the fitness boom of the seventies carried cycling in its wake. It became a leisure activity, a tie not to poverty but betterment. And because leisure is the luxury of those with time and money, it was a sport for the better-off. Cyclists weren't butcher's boys, like Coppi, or sons of railway workers, like Hinault. They came from real-estate families, like Greg LeMond, or university teachers, like Andy Hampsten. They were odd, but they weren't paupers.

That helps explain the success the U.S. has had despite no modern tradition of racing, and in countries an ocean away. European countries may be more successful in relation to their population, but the U.S. has become big. Britain, which never stopped cycling, has yet to field a successful team, let alone win the Tour. The U.S. did that three times in a decade.

The first success was Jonathon Boyer, a thoughtful and determined man who rode the 1973 junior world championship and used a part-time job while he was still at school to get to the AC Boulogne-Billancourt in western Paris. The ACBB was a school for professionals, particularly Peugeot. It had helped Tom Simpson, Shay Elliott, Stephen Roche, Phil Anderson ("Skippy" to the French, after a TV kangaroo), and Robert Millar. Boyer joined not Peugeot but Lejeune-BP for a reputed $650 a month. His backers were a Parisian bike company in the sport in a small way for years and a huge oil company which had co-sponsored numerous teams, including Poulidor's Mercier. Boyer's manager was the former Tour runner-up Henry Anglade, a bossy little man nicknamed "Napoléon." His team-mates included Lucien van Impe, who had won the Tour the year before Boyer joined.

American journalist Ed Pavelka ran **Velo-News** from offices in Brattleboro, Vermont. He saw the second glory time of American racing, from Jacques Boyer to Greg LeMond. Now, he says, Boyer and his pioneering rides are all but forgotten. And LeMond, of course, has been eclipsed by Lance Armstrong. Pavelka is no stranger to long-distance riding himself, having twice ridden Paris–Brest–Paris.

The plan was that Boyer would ride the Tour straight away. But a crash and then a stomach virus from the world championship in Venezuela put him out. It took a year, a trip home to Carmel, California, and a regime as a vegetarian to recover. By then Lejeune was over. Puch was the highest he could go, but there was no van Impe to support and a small team can be good for an ambitious rider. Boyer rode a good Tour of Switzerland and then in appalling weather beneath Mont Blanc, he finished fifth in the world championship on the last Sunday of August 1989.

The course was said to have been selected for Hinault. It went along a valley in Sallanches, up the Domency climb, then fast down the other side. Over and over for 168 miles. Hinault says in *Le Peloton des Souvenirs*, "I was so excited that I went three nights without sleeping. I was on the boil... I almost struck a woman who wanted my autograph and picked a bad moment to ask me. She insisted and I gave her a mouthful... Fortunately I slept like a child the night before the race."

Boyer was never likely to win, but even to finish was something. For an American to come fifth was astonishing. If that sounds patronizing, remember it had never happened, nor anything like it. And now it had happened in a race of attrition, where Hinault had ordered his team to push hard enough from the start to send dozens back to the pits as soon as possible.

Boyer stayed with me in the spring of 1978 when I lived in Belgium. He spent hours boiling the curiously-smelling vegetarian meals that caused further interest in the meat-eating peloton. We went to the Omloop van het Waasland at Kemzeke, near Antwerp, which turned out to be Eddy Merckx's last race. I met Merckx on my way to speak to Boyer in Sallanches and asked what he made of Boyer.

"I think he has a very great talent and that America will be the land of the future for cycling," he said with practiced diplomacy.

"Because of the money or the talent?" I asked, conscious there was more of the first than the second.

"The money certainly," Merckx said, now keener on getting out of the rain than talking to me. I walked with him. "But I think the day will come soon when we will see much more talent from America as well. I have no doubt that cycling has a big future there." I teased him that he was being over-polite, conscious that I was writing for *Velo-News*, then still a struggling newspaper in Vermont.

"No, no," he insisted, "I think we'll see it happen."

Others also saw potential. To ride well in a world championship is always good. To do it with no worthwhile team, within grasp of the podium, in France, and to survive Hinault... all that is good indeed. Jean De Gribaldy, a grey-haired eccentric, furniture millionaire, and former rider who styled himself Count, stood at the back of the press seats. He'd dabbled in many teams, including Belgium's Flandria, although not always with conspicuous success. By then I was all but campaigning on Boyer's behalf. De Gribaldy smiled like an old uncle and said, "I think we would be interested in talking about a place for him."

Fortunately the offer came instead from Cyrille Guimard, and Guimard was boss of Renault-Gitane and Hinault. Guimard was an interesting character and first of the modern team managers. His story is that he became *maillot jaune* in 1972, despite being a sprinter. Proving he could keep the jersey through the mountains cost him dear. His knee gave out in the Pyrénées and he couldn't walk. Doctors worked on him every night, but he still had to be carried to his bike. Two days before Paris he couldn't even pedal, and he had to abandon on the night before the finish, while he was second overall and the best sprinter. He never rode the Tour again.

Boyer was 25, tall and personable, well known in France, a good French-speaker, and shrewd enough to wear a stetson when it suited him. The Tour encouraged him to wear stars and stripes rather than a Renault jersey — something that otherwise would have meant a fine. America, not used to one of its own doing well, started to fancy in 1981 that this deeply religious man could even win. Boyer knew he wouldn't. If he'd had the talent, he didn't have the job. His rôle was to shovel for Hinault. And Hinault wasn't about to let anybody, even an American, stand in his light. What Geoffrey Nicholson called this "slightly dandified" American was a constant fascination, alternately colorful and serious. This occasional earnestness became a talking point. The reporter Dennis Donovan says journalists took pity on his seeming loneliness in a French team and suggested they might procure girlie mags for him.

"Thank you, but no," Boyer reputedly said. "I have my Bible and that is all I require." By nightfall the Dutch had got hold of the story and, biggest gossips on the race, they'd spread it around the world.

Boyer rode well. He came ninth on the longest day — 259 km from Le Mans to Aulnay-sous-Bois — and wheeled to a halt in 32nd place in the center of Paris. American cycling had come a lot farther than the 3,753 km he'd pedaled from Nice. So had Australian cycling. Phil Anderson, born in London and with cycling's most magnificent teeth, had clung to Hinault over the Plat d'Adet and became Down Under's first maillot jaune. Hinault, unamused, took it back next day.

Pioneers come too early. Anderson had Opperman and others to buoy him up. Boyer was alone. Ed Pavelka, then editor of *Velo-News* and later of *Bicycling*, told me, "Boyer was too far ahead of the curve — a lone U.S. eagle in the Tour. Those of us in cycling were in awe, but that's about as far as it went for his celebrity. I remember *Sports Illustrated* doing a feature story about him. This seemed huge at the time because finally someone noticed. Boyer broke major ground for U.S. cycling, but I'm willing to bet that the average European would recognize his name before the average American."

It wasn't the last time he'd be denied his place in the sun. Boyer rode as a professional from 1977 to 1987. He rode Paris–Roubaix six times, six Tours of Switzerland, three Giros, and five Tours. He also looked like winning the 1982 world championship at Goodwood, a horse-racing town in green hills close to Brighton, England. But in defeat came the start of a bitter rift in American cycling.

Boyer started the sprint as the break topped the hill just before the finish. There, too, were Italy's Beppe Saronni and two other English-speakers, Greg LeMond and Ireland's Sean Kelly. Boyer opened a gap and many thought the American Tour pioneer was about to become the U.S.'s first world road champion. The notion was encouraged by one of those curious pauses when nobody knew what to do. Boyer soared ahead. Saronni, LeMond, and Kelly were all watching each other. Saronni was worried about Kelly, never yet a world champion but geographically as close to becoming one in Ireland as he was ever likely to be. LeMond, less a sprinter, was tied by Boyer's attack.

And then something odd happened. Look at photographs and you'll see a smile starting on Saronni's lips. He's looking not at Kelly but at LeMond, whose American jersey is — to Saronni's disbelief but enormous joy — about to start chasing Boyer's. Saronni sprinted off his wheel, LeMond followed him, and then Kelly. Boyer, with surprise on his side but a 500 m sprint, had his championship taken by his own team-mate. He came not first but tenth. And worse, LeMond didn't win either. It was the Italian national anthem they played at the presentation.

LeMond, only 20, said he owed nothing to Boyer or to America. The man hadn't even won a professional race, he said. And the U.S. team had been no more than individuals in the same colors. There was no manager. Nobody, least of all America, had paid him to ride or met his travel costs. He was a professional. Racing was his job. His living depended on whether he won or lost. That day, both lost.

I found Boyer sitting on a low wall in the American pits. Nobody was speaking to him. I soon found out why.

"How do you feel about that?" I asked.

"HOW THE HELL DO YOU THINK I FEEL?" he snapped.

I took it the interview was over.

19
News from Chambéry

A ND THE NEW world champion... we've just heard from Chambéry... the new world champion..." the *speaker* builds the tension, and you can see the little crowd, from the *boulangerie* down to the entrance to the fairground, shuffling, waiting for the name.

"*Le nouveau champion du monde 1989, c'est...*" and again we wait, more nervously now — "*c'est Greg LeMond!*" Two hundred miles to the east, where the race has taken place, this is undoubtedly big news. In a small village, where a bike race marked just another weekend en *fête*, it falls like a wet sandwich. The crowd is as talkative as a Trappist reunion.

"*C'est Greg LeMond qui a battu notre Laurent Fignon à Paris, cet Américain formidable, il est devenu le champion du monde pour la deuxième fois!*"

The French are corporately unmoved. He may have a French name (it's odd how many have — Boyer, Roche, LeMond...) but he isn't French, and that's all that matters. They go back to matters in hand, in this case *la deuxième edition du Tour National Féminin du Tarn-et-Garonne.*

The French were always fascinated by LeMond, but not so much that they hoped he'd beat a Frenchman. No Frenchman is ever likely to do that, although they marveled as much as anyone when LeMond clipped on triathlon bars to win the Tour by eight seconds from Fignon. What they liked was the *joie de vivre* they thought they'd get with Boyer. Boyer had panache, but LeMond's bursting smile was a joy in a nation that doesn't smile instinctively. So was the way, the al-

141

most sacrilegious way, he was photographed sipping champagne in bed beneath a Stars and Stripes.

As a kid he wrote his ambitions on a sheet of paper and kept it in his desk. The wish was to win the Olympics — which he couldn't because the U.S. didn't send a team in 1980 — the Tour, and a world championship. The acne-dotted boy I met in the pits at the world championship near Heerlen in Holland became world junior champion in a controversial race in 1979, turned professional in 1981, won the Tour de l'Avenir in 1982, and then became world champion in 1983, the year he also won the Super Prestige Pernod.

I remember Phil Corley, a British professional champion, putting down *Cycling* and saying "Either they've got this Le Mond guy all hyped up or he's the next Merckx." I've left the gap in LeMond because that, in those days, was how strangers wrote and pronounced it. Well, LeMond was never Merckx but, with three Tours, he was no lightweight either. I also remember the former British champion Neil Dykes saying that wherever he went in Belgium, mystified locals would ask if he knew this Greg LeMond.

"LeMond had come to Belgium for a week or something as a completely unknown junior, so I'd never heard of him either," he said from his home in Colorado, "and he'd won everything he'd ridden,

Bernard Hinault said he would help LeMond win the Tour de France. His method, though, was to ride at the front and defy LeMond to hang on. If he could do it, he would win the Tour. If he couldn't, he wasn't worthy of it. The battle on the Alpe d'Huez in 1986 ended in a truce, and the race with an American victory. But the two don't exchange Christmas cards.

day after day for a week. The rest of us thought we were doing well to get into the prizes, and there were local guys who never did. And then in comes this American who wins everything and goes home again. They'd heard of him all over Belgium and came up asking who the hell he was. Years afterwards I went to hear Greg talking. He said that that was the moment he realized he had an extraordinary talent and I thought, 'Yes, and everybody else realized it then as well.'"

LeMond came third in his first Tour in 1984 and won the white jersey as best new pro. That was how the French liked it — novelty but nothing to upset a Tour de France for France. Fignon had won it and he may not have had Hinault's strength but he was good enough. Hinault the Badger — nobody knew whether he got the nickname for his tenacity, his grey-flecked hair or a rumored pet — rode on a new team called La Vie Claire. It had been set up by what the business pages called the "colorful" Bernard Tapie, whose rags-to-riches career as a millionaire, government minister, and European parliamentarian collapsed a decade later, when he was declared bankrupt and charged with rigging a soccer match and interfering with witnesses.

Tapie took on LeMond as Hinault's apprentice for 1985, or to stop his getting in the way of the fifth win that would put Hinault among the gods. You chose the interpretation you preferred. Either way, no arrangement was more likely to end in tears. In 1985, Hinault and LeMond agreed to work for whichever was better placed. Hinault was 31 but he was clever. He won the prologue at Plumelec and then the first time-trial by an astonishing 2:20. He had LeMond strategically clamped. And that's how it would have stayed had Hinault not crashed just before the Pyrénées.

A broken nose is not what you want in the mountains. Hinault struggled up the climb of Luz-Ardiden, unable to hold Stephen Roche, his greatest threat. LeMond stuck by his agreement and held Roche's wheel as he went into the clouds with Eduardo Chozas of Spain. Then he realized he was stronger than both Roche and the Spaniard. Hinault was more than a minute behind, and if LeMond could win the Tour then Hinault could still be runner-up. Inspired, he called for his Swiss manager, Paul Köchli.

"Can I go?" he shouted. Köchli refused.

"You can't ride with Roche. You can't attack," he said. "Hinault's coming up. You've got to wait for him."

LeMond began arguing.

"How far back is he?"

At first Köchli wouldn't say. When LeMond pressed him, he said 40 or 45 seconds. The argument was still going when Luis Herrera joined them. Roche despaired as the increasingly angry words took the sting out of the break. Reluctantly LeMond obeyed, the break fizzled, and a group of 16 caught them, Hinault not among them. That night LeMond was in foul mood. The "45 seconds" had turned out 1:15 at the finish, and LeMond had already delayed the break a further minute on Köchli's orders. He had been not only misled but denied the Tour. Tapie sought him out at a party and promised him next year's Tour if he'd give this one to Hinault. LeMond had little choice; he stood beneath Hinault on the podium in Paris and did his best to smile.

A year passed and the two returned in 1986 for a counterclockwise and particularly mountainous Tour. Hinault set out, not to deny LeMond, but not to make it easy either. Publicly, his view had been that a sixth Tour wasn't important. Privately, it's hard to imagine he believed it, still less that he felt happy at the risk of being dominated, not simply by LeMond, but by the Colombians, whom the Tour had imported as part of its globalization and for whom all those mountains were surely intended.

He attacked so hard on the first day in the Pyrénées that the field splintered. LeMond lost four minutes and Laurent Fignon the whole race, 11 minutes down. It was unsettling to say the least, and baffling for LeMond. What had that promise from Tapie been worth? Was there some hint even then that the man was less than uncomplicated? LeMond must still have been trying to work it out when Hinault tried again next day on the Tourmalet and on the col d'Aspin to Superbagnères — and snapped. Now LeMond could smile at last: he had the yellow jersey.

An uneasy truce boiled over five days later over the Galibier and the Croix-de-Fer to Alpe d'Huez. Hinault attacked, LeMond refusing to retaliate or drop. Thousands lined the roads, waving, shouting, running alongside only to jump clear of the following motorcycles. And then, as Hinault realized just before the finish that the American wasn't going to crack, LeMond rode alongside and put an arm around his shoulders. Then he let Hinault win. What had happened? What had been said? What had been offered and accepted?

Hinault said he'd been gracious, that he'd passed on the crown by risking the initiative of the attack, towing his team-mate through the mountains and winning him the Tour. It was a line the French press loved. Hinault had shown himself stronger, won the stage, kept his promise, been magnanimous, and honored the Republic. For a long time LeMond said nothing. Then he said Hinault had asked for one last victory, a final win in the mountains. The Frenchman's patronizing hurt him. He could have left Hinault for five minutes, he'd learned to see through him. Years later he added: "It almost burned me out of cycling, that little episode. I didn't even feel like racing the following year. It was like being burned by your brother. The thing is that Hinault wasn't your typical team-mate. He was a guy I idolized." The two have been cool ever since.

Hinault says in *Memories of the Peloton*:

LeMond's ride into Paris brought him the smallest winning margin the Tour has ever known. Laurent Fignon, never famous for his good humor, was even less amused when LeMond used what was then the mildly comical idea of tri-bars to beat him by eight seconds. Finishing with a time-trial was a tradition from the start but the Champs Elysées finish was new. It secured France's most famous street for the Tour for the foreseeable future. Just alongside it is a tree given by the people of America to the people of France to mark the American bicentennial in 1989. It's doubtful LeMond had time to notice it.

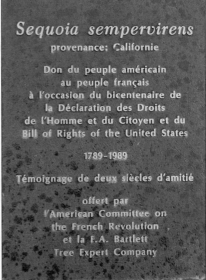

Sequoia sempervirens
provenance: Californie

Don du peuple américain
au peuple français
à l'occasion du bicentenaire de
la Déclaration des Droits
de l'Homme et du Citoyen et du
Bill of Rights of the United States

1789-1989

Témoignage de deux siècles d'amitié

offert par
l'American Committee on
the French Revolution
et la F.A. Bartlett
Tree Expert Company

I'd given my word to Greg LeMond that I'd help him win and that's what I did. A promise is a promise and I don't go back on my word. I tried to wear out rivals to help him, but I never attacked him personally... It wasn't my fault that he didn't understand this. When I think of the things he's said since the race ended, I wonder whether I was right not to attack him. He claims that he didn't need my help. Why? Does he think he could have won alone?

I've worked for colleagues all my life without having the problems I had with Greg LeMond. He's a top-class rider but he seems to unstable, incapable of accepting the responsibility that the race leader needs. He worries too much and can't get on with people... Greg LeMond still has the hardest lesson to learn: humility. Americans seem to me to be lacking in humility.

For LeMond, that was nearly the end of the story. His brother-in-law shot him in the back accidentally during a turkey-hunt near Sacramento the following April and he lay in a coma for two weeks. Many thought he wouldn't live, and nobody expected him on a bike. But you don't win the Tour if you can't suffer. He got over a knee operation, then an appendectomy, and finally began training in September, although he concedes it was too soon.

"Nearly 60 percent of my blood volume was gone and that takes months to get back," he said. "I remember going back to Europe at the end of August and only being able to make it one mile into a race. I was doing it because under my contract with PDM it was contingent that I would start racing again in '88. Plus my contract with La Vie Claire required that I race x number of days in '87. If I hadn't raced again that year, they would have been able to cancel my contract. So I was forced to go back."

It was painful, but to everyone's amazement he turned up at the Giro in 1989, sometimes struggling but also chasing in Lech Piasecki of Poland in the time-trial. Most felt sorry for him. Imagine having been the best and then to be humiliated. He had no appendix; his liver and kidneys were permanently damaged. It was an impossible task. The Giro was not a success, yet he came through it.

In 1989 he came to the Tour with drawling American French he'd learned in his wasted years. It was just the first oddity of a curious Tour. They began when Pedro Delgado lost 2:54 by signing autographs instead of going to the prologue; they continued when

LeMond won the 73 km time-trial at Rennes on stage five and prompted *L'Équipe* to yell *"La Résurrection!"* and they ended with LeMond and Fignon 50 seconds apart at the start of the time-trial into Paris.

It was the epic finish of the modern era. Just 24.5 km would decide the Tour, a quarter of a century after Anquetil and Poulidor. Fignon used a standard time-trial bike; LeMond again fitted tri-bars, 90-degree extensions to his handlebars that were so misunderstood when they arrived in Europe that one magazine dismissed them as a crazy American way to let triathletes lounge on their bikes. The notion of wind-trimming didn't sink in until later, and Fignon learned the lesson eight seconds too late. He also had a cyst on his backside, something he didn't care to talk about before the race ended.

The two had scrapped all through the Tour and they were the last starters of the 138 survivors. LeMond started two minutes in front, riding in his novel Superman crouch. Fignon left off his helmet because of the warmth and let his ponytail fall down his back. He rode uncomfortably but frighteningly fast.

LeMond had five seconds after three miles, enough to shock Fignon into asking confirmation from his manager. At six miles they were on the bank of the river Seine, Fignon losing almost two seconds a kilometer. He was 18 seconds back but he could still win the Tour. LeMond at this rate would win the stage by 46 seconds but not the race. The road rose and dipped under the bridges across the river. LeMond stayed in 55×12, tugging his tri-bars; Fignon got out of the saddle and moved across the road to use the crowd as a windbreak. It was a symptom of the end or perhaps the cause. Nobody knows which, but he'd lost 37 seconds as he turned on to the traffic-worn cobbles of the Place de la Concorde and the Champs Elysées. The two crossed in opposite directions.

LeMond averaged 54.545 km/h, the fastest Tour time-trial longer than 20 km. He stood staring at the clock, chest pumping, counting the seconds until Fignon's arrival. At the moment he won the Tour he let out a whoop and hugged anybody available to be hugged. Even dignitaries from the American embassy across the road yelled with him. Fignon had lost by eight seconds after 3,285 km.

Later that year LeMond won the world championship for the second time, and in 1990 a third Tour. He wore yellow again in 1991, but by then the crown had passed to Miguel Indurain. In his last years he rode little and concentrated on the Tour and the world championship. Merckx accused him of disrespect by not riding the classics. Others agreed. But Merckx was of an era when, for all the money, professionals were cyclists first and businessmen afterwards. They expected to ride from one end of the season to the other.

LeMond saw it as a trade. He came from a country with no modern tradition of racing but a lot of experience of stars exploiting their attraction. He said, "Bernard Hinault was getting as much press for Renault as Renault's Formula One team, yet they were spending $50 million on the car-racing team and only $2 million on the bike-racing team. Hinault, one of the most famous people in France, was only making $150,000 a year, while Alain Prost was making $8 or $9 million a year. There were inequalities that needed addressing."

Now LeMond is himself a car-racer, involved with Formula Ford 2000 since the day a friend persuaded him to try a driving school. Car racing is stimulating, he told Bryan Malessa of *Bicyclist*, "but even when I'm racing a lot, it doesn't take the same passion that cycling professionally requires." He stepped off amid continuing taunts that he was old, lazy, always tired. It was frustrating for a man who only a few years ago hadn't been expected to live.

Sometimes, he admits, he says to himself: "My God, I'm never going to race in the Tour de France again." He still feels sentimental when he sees it. He was diagnosed in 1994 as having mitochondrial myopathy, a degenerative muscle disease. He still has five pellets in the lining of his heart, five in his liver and in his spine. Europeans, he says, never realized the gravity of the accident.

Meanwhile the crown has passed. In 1999 Lance Armstrong closed the millennium with a new American victory; and he, too, had overcome a medical catastrophe, in his case testicular cancer.

20

Blood on the Tracks

T HEY'D blanked out Fabio's name. That's when it really sank in."
So said the New Zealander Stephen Swart in Tarbes on July 19,
1995, when the Tour came to terms with death among its own. Fabio
Casartelli was a few days short of his 25th birthday, a jobbing professional still to make the transition from his Olympic championship in
Barcelona in 1992. On July 18 he had a new titanium bike to start the
Tour's 15th day. An hour later he was lying smashed on the side of the
col de Portet d'Aspet. It was the first climb of the day and he'd ridden
just 34 km.

Casartelli, six feet tall and close to 170 pounds, was dropping off
the hill at 55 mph. The descent would have taken him down 4,000
feet. The road swung left, with a ravine to the right fenced by con-
crete blocks designed to stop cars. Casartelli, Breukink, Baldinger,
Perini, Rezze, and Museeuw all fell, Rezze tumbling down the hillside
and struggling back only minutes later. The others rode off, but
Casartelli had skidded across the road on his left and hit one of the
blocks. His blood ran across the road. Gérard Porte and Gérard
Nicolet, the two doctors, got him into a helicopter, but his heart
stopped three times before he reached hospital in Tarbes. He died of
brain damage and the news struck hard, not only in Italy but in America, where his presence on an American team was second best to nationality.

Michel Disteldorf, the doctor who examined the body, said a helmet might have prevented some injuries. Others said it was hard to
see how. If Casartelli had hit the block at only 20 mph, about a third

149

of his riding speed, the impact would have been too great for anything but a motorcyclist's helmet. Cyrille Guimard, manager of the Castorama team, said, "If you crash at 65 km/h, it doesn't matter whether you're wearing a helmet or not."

The trust fund set up after his death soon looked like reaching $250,000 for Casartelli's son, Marco. The Motorola manager, Jim Ochowicz, told me from team headquarters in Milwaukee that checks had ranged from $5 to $1,000, almost all from within the U.S. There's now a memorial a hundred meters from the site, as close as it proved practical to build it. It's a winged wheel in white marble, on a grey marble base on which is set a sundial. Ochowicz said it symbolised "his life, his Olympic victory, and his death." It was paid for by Motorola and dedicated the following November, on the anniversary of the end of World War One. Ochowicz said, "You can't see it from the actual spot, but you would if you took a couple of paces." Tour organisers and members of the Casartelli fund travelled there on the rest day of the 1999 race to pay homage.

It takes a second glance to notice the damage to the bike on which Fabio Casartelli became the Tour's third rider to die. The steering is bent out of line and the paint is scratched, but there's little more. It stands on a shelf beneath the curved ceiling of the Madonna del Ghisallo chapel near Casartelli's home in Como. In front of it is one of Eddy Merckx's machines.

The Tour came in for criticism. Casartelli died early in the stage. Although Richard Virenque crossed the line unaware of what had happened, the Festina team preferring not to disturb his solo ride, most knew what had happened within 30 minutes. Several wept as they rode. Virenque still didn't know when he went to the podium. But the Tour organisers did. *Gazzetta dello Sport* called the celebrations "grotesque, offensive, and unforgivable." Even the Vatican regretted that "everything went ahead as if that fatal blood on the tar did not exist." It became a circus of bad taste. TV viewers began complaining they hadn't seen the crash, so television compensated by showing the dead man in a bag on its freezer shelf. Next day *L'Équipe*'s cartoon showed a cyclist riding a mountain to heaven; a spectator is shouting: "It's Fabio!"

Casartelli's body arrived at Milan airport next day to be delivered to Albese, near Lake Como, home to Casartelli, his wife Annalisa, and four-month-old Marco. The riders gave them the $100,000 of next day's prizes, the Tour the same amount. A fund opened at the Harris Trust and Savings Bank in Chicago. The Tour continued as usual that morning in Tarbes. Or almost as usual. Most expected Motorola to pull out. Ochowicz wouldn't force the riders either way. The riders arrived late next morning, their car carrying the bent bike hung with black ribbons. The crowd applauded, then stood for a minute before Lance Armstrong led the team and the race on their way.

"The first 24 hours were the worst," Ochowicz said.

Casartelli's was the Tour's third acknowledged death. In 1935, the Spaniard Francisco Cepeda fell down a cliff on the Galibier near Bourg d'Oisans and died three days later in hospital in Grenoble, and in 1967 Tom Simpson died on Mont Ventoux. Cepeda is all but forgotten but riders cross themselves as they pass Simpson's memorial and they stopped when they next passed Casartelli's.

Cycling is a relatively dangerous sport, especially where speed and tricky courses are combined. World champion André Raynaud died during a motor-paced race on Antwerp track in 1937, Richard Depoorter crashed into a tunnel on the Tour of Switzerland and died in 1948, Camille Danguillaume was hit by a motorcycle in the French national championship in 1950, and so the list goes on, including Stan Ockers and his fatal crash on the Antwerp track in 1956, José Samyn who hit a programme seller during a kermesse in Belgium, and Jempi Monseré, the previous year's world amateur champion, who died after he hit a car during a race in Belgium in his first year as a professional.

There's a chapel on the Tour of Lombardy, the Madonna del Ghisallo, that has become a shrine to the world's greatest cyclists. It stands on a six-mile climb north-east of Como. Inside is one of Coppi's bikes and others from Eddy Merckx, Felice Gimondi, Alfredo Binda, and Gino Bartali. So too is the machine on which Francesco Moser broke the world hour record. Small plaques remember dead cyclists otherwise long forgotten. That is where you can find Casartelli's Olympic jersey and the bike he was riding when he died. The forks are bent, the front wheel damaged and the paint scratched, but otherwise not much suggests the scale of the impact.

The Tour has long had to handle scandal, tragedy, and excess. In 1978 it seemed unreasonably difficult, and by day 12 a revolution was waiting to happen. Many riders reckon to get only six hours' sleep a night after the first week, enough to make anybody bad-tempered even without the racing and the plane and train transfers of which the organisers had grown fond. When revolution broke, the riders had had a hard day and hadn't recovered by the time they got to their hotels at 9 p.m. Worse, their alarms would be going at 4:30 a.m. to prepare for a split day to Toulouse. They would race from Tarbes to a little town called Valence d'Agen and then in the afternoon from there to Toulouse. In all they were in for 254 km, in a split stage that all riders detest, after little sleep and scant time to eat and be massaged. And, of course, they had the transfer to Tarbes, something they disliked even more.

With hindsight, the reaction was predictable. The race rode for 157 km at 12 mph, while Jacques Goddet begged the riders to get on with the racing and discuss the issues afterwards. When they declined, he threatened to withhold their prizes, then said he'd still award them if they raced at least the last 30 km. In Valence, a market town of about 14,000 in which nothing much happens, the mayor was growing increasingly angry. His town had taken a lot of trouble and spent a lot of money on its big moment. It didn't want it all thrown away. He was beside himself when the bunch climbed off and began to walk to the line. He shouted at Hinault, who had been called into the front row as national champion, and he shouted at Michel Pollentier and Freddy Maertens, the mountain and points leaders beside him. Hinault tried to explain the riders' views and got branded as a ringleader because of it. The mayor wasn't consoled but he did at least get a promise that the riders would return to Valence and ride a race for no fees.

"You treat us like animals, not athletes," riders protested. But Goddet stuck firm, insisting "it's necessary to keep an inhuman side to the Tour; excess is necessary." How excessive it could become became clear on the Alpe d'Huez shortly afterwards. Michel Pollentier had been in the front row of the walking strike, and now he was back in the news alone.

Pollentier was Belgium's national champion, a balding 27-year-old whose pleasantness off his bike was cancelled by his style on it. He rode twisted, contorted, and cramped, and he scuttled up the Alpe to take the yellow jersey. What happened next was farce. Race officials called three riders to the drug test. Along with Pollentier, they wanted José Nazabal and Antoine Guttierez. Nazabal gave his sample but must have guessed the result because he left the race that night. He and Pollentier were waiting in the doctor's trailer when Guttierez was

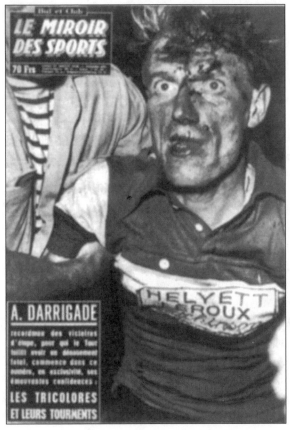

André Darrigade came close to dying in the Tour. Going for yet another sprint win at Bordeaux, he piled into a man who stepped on to the track. Their heads smashed together and the man was dead before he hit the ground. Darrigade, although cut and bloody, wasn't seriously hurt.

discovered with a bottle and tubes wrapped round him. He had un-contaminated urine in the rubber bottle, which he could keep warm in his armpit. A tube ran inside his jersey to his shorts or the cuff of a long sleeve. Squeezing the bottle gave the impression of urinating.

The doctor tugged Pollentier's jersey and found he too was similarly prepared. Both were disqualified, fined, and suspended. Sensation was all the greater because Pollentier had won alone, not by chance. That guaranteed a test and he must have been convinced of the ruse. The assumption was that it had been field-tested many times within the sport. Pollentier had taken amphetamine.

I met him one afternoon in Keiem, a village near Dixmuide. He lived in Dodepaardenstraat — Dead Horses Street — which had a black irony. I can't say he seemed embarrassed, but then a decade is a long time to come to terms with foolishness.

"They were very sympathetic here," he said, wearing a chequered cotton shirt and sipping from a bottle of water. His championship certificates hung on the wall and his children played in front of an enormous TV. "There were thousands of letters from all sorts of countries, wishing me well and telling me to fight it and get back again. I did my two-month suspension, and of course it fell in the criterium period, so that made it more expensive for me because I couldn't ride them. But when I went to watch, they gave me a round of applause. Certainly nobody laughed at me or anything like that."

All sorts of rumours surrounded the day — that a new doctor was doing his job properly; that the Tour was out to stop a Belgian leading; that someone wanted to get him personally. Pollentier said most of those things himself at his hotel. He even named a rider who'd lost a stage to avoid a test, and said half the bunch was using "products," although he wouldn't say they were drugs. Such is the contorted talk of professional cycling, I reminded him. He shrugged. "Who knows what the truth is or what led to it all? It all seemed very strange, but it was also a long time ago." The matter was closed. But not for the Tour. Pollentier was only small beer compared to what came next.

The 13th stage of 1988 was a 38 km time-trial through the foothills of the Alps. Pedro Delgado was riding his sixth Tour, wearing the yellow jersey he had taken from the Canadian Steve Bauer. Delgado was popular in Spain, where the government once broke session to watch him on television, although a pain to sponsors and organisers with whom he'd spend hours negotiating expenses for driving to races. He kept a notebook detailing prizes to the peseta.

The reporter credited with unearthing the scandal that broke around him is Patrick Chêne, of French television. Delgado had given his sample to Jean Court, the drug-check official, and it had gone to Professor Jean-Pierre Lafarge in Clichy. On July 19, Lafarge watched the equipment twitch at precisely the point that indicated probenecide. Probenicide masks anabolic steroids in urine. At 7 p.m. on Thursday July 21, Chêne began Antenne 2's Journal du Tour with the announcement that Delgado had been found positive. The Tour neither denied nor confirmed it. It was such a scoop that neither Court nor the doctor, Gérard Porte, had heard of it. In fact Porte was furious that Chêne could make such a claim on television. But Antenne 2 trusted its sources. And it was right.

That night, Delgado was on the interview programme that followed the live coverage. Questioned by Alain Vernon, he said he had indeed taken probenicide. He named the doctor in France who had suggested it. Yet there was a twist. Probenicide was banned only by the IOC, the Olympic body. It wasn't due to be banned by cycling's UCI until August, after the Tour had ended. Delgado still insists he was innocent. He won the race but the victory will always carry questions.

At least he said what he took. If you go to St. Germain du Plain in Paris, you may still find a shop marked *Établissement Rachel Dard — Cycles et Fabrication*. In 1976, Rachel Dard was a promising profes-

Coppi, Bartali, Binda, Indurain. Their yellow and rainbow jerseys stand together in the Madonna del Ghisallo chapel, surrounded by trade jerseys, Giro jerseys and Olympic rings. The chapel is open most of the day with no fee asked save a voluntary donation.

sional on the Peugeot team. Maurice De Muer was the boss, and Bernard Thévenet and Jean-Pierre Danguillaume among the riders. That autumn, the team was riding the Étoile des Espoirs in France, with Jean-Luc Vandenbroucke first overall and Dard among the stage winners. The race got to Dax, and Dard and his team-mate Bourreau were called to the drug test. They were caught with a Pollentier pear.

The doctor running the tests was Bruno Chaumont, a new and amiable young man who rumour said would pass tests with a nod. But he didn't. He was idealistic and believed in sportsmanship. Dard, particularly, was distraught. Not only had he lost all he'd won but Peugeot would fire him, his salary would end, and there was little chance another team would look at a first-year professional who'd already got himself into trouble.

He hoped he had persuaded Chaumont that he didn't deserve the consequences and that the reports would be torn up. But then it occurred to him that Chaumont still had the test bottles and would return them to the lab in Paris. They were empty, of course, because Dard had been caught before he'd filled them. But they should have been full. It was all very well scrapping the test report, but empty bottles were as condemning as drugged full ones.

Dard and his team-mate Bernard Croyet followed the doctor to Dax. Seeing him board a train to Paris, they jumped in their car and raced it back to the capital. Dard was waiting at the Gare d'Austerlitz when Chaumont stepped out. The begging began again. And this time Chaumont relented and smashed the bottles.

There the story would have ended had *L'Équipe* not run an exposé of drugs in cycling. Chaumont began having regrets. He went to the paper and his tale appeared next morning. The French cycling association was embarrassed and retaliated with fines and suspensions all round. By now, Dard had nothing to lose. He told *L'Équipe* the dates and details of the drugs he'd been given. This embarrassed everyone even more and the sport didn't dare punish him further for fear of making him a scapegoat. He sat out his suspension and returned to Peugeot, where De Muer allowed him a few minor races. The next year he tried again on another team and then stopped for good.

Sometimes disruption has come from outside. Spanish terrorists set fire to journalists' cars, including one belonging to Britain's Channel 4 TV, a fact it reported with a mix of wonderment and resentment. Striking steel workers stopped the team time-trial at Denain in 1982;

the organisers couldn't restart it and abandoned a stage for the first time. Farm workers followed suite shortly afterwards and before long stopping races became a hobby in a land in which workers strike first and negotiate afterwards. Riders tired so much of being showered with leaflets or halted that Hinault once entertainingly drew back a fist in Paris–Nice and walloped the nearest available *communard*. The race then set off again and the unions chose different ways to protest. Until 1999, anyway, when striking firemen stopped the race and a bunch of hooligans pelted the bunch with stink bombs.

21
A Day in the Life

I MET PETER POST at his house in Cobe Ritsemahof, a street in Amstelveen. The town runs into Amsterdam in Holland, and his address was always published as the place to write for the Raleigh team, which he ran for 12 years, and then for the Panasonic squad that replaced it. His first professional win was the Chicago six-day in 1957 and his last the Frankfurt six-day 18 years — and 65 six-day wins — later. It was a record that stood until 1979. He won a wet Paris–Roubaix in record time in 1964 and his 45.13 km/h was for nearly 30 years not simply the fastest Roubaix but the fastest classic ever.

He then became one of the sport's most successful managers. Raleigh won 15 world championships, five World Cups, a Tour de France, and 77 of its stages. It won the Giro d'Italia, 37 classics, and 55 national championships. It's possible Post knows what he's talking about.

His house was single-story, light-colored, and modern. A red Mercedes stood outside. His wife told me he apologized for lateness and that he'd be there within moments. When he arrived, he was as bear-like as he looked on his bike and open friendliness hid the iron side that led one rider to describe him as "hard as stone." A scar below one eye illustrated the danger of his trade and his face had that battered look of an ex-boxer, the expression of a million hard nights in darkened stadiums.

Politely, he marveled that I had cycled 60 miles to see him, then turned on Dutch television's teletext service to tell me the pound had fallen a cent against the guilder. He seemed more put out about it than I was. The pound had been losing a cent against the guilder for as long as I could remember. For a while we exchanged pleasantries, and then I said, "People say you're not the easiest man to get along with. In fact, they say you're a good friend but a terrible enemy." I remembered British riders drafted into the team when it started in the 1970s coming home across the North Sea grumbling at how they'd been treated. Other teams called it *Panzer Gruppe Post* or shortened TI-Raleigh to *Tirgruppe*, or firing squad.

Hennie Kuiper had his best years at Raleigh and became world champion in its colors, riding with rainbow-colored handlebar tape. I called at his house in Putte by the Belgian border and asked whether, results aside, he'd been happy in the team he was adamant.

"No! Not at all."

"Why?"

He waited and then with characteristic stammer said, "My character and Peter Post's character are totally different. I was still a youngster. And when you're young and you have some sort of problem, you need to discuss it. But that was almost impossible. He's as hard as stone. I can be hard as well but the difference was much too big." I doubt they exchange Christmas cards.

That was what I was thinking about when I put it to Post. He shrugged and recrossed his feet. After a while he said, "I'm not always the easiest on myself either. I don't think it's possible to be a nice guy in cycling these days. And if you're responsible for a team, for the money, then you've got to say something to a rider." Among those things, according to Gerald O'Donovan, his boss back in England, was a budget so tight that "riders needed a receipt in triplicate if they bought a bottle of Coke." When Brits complained that Post gave them broken-down equipment to hasten them home, the truth is more that the whole team had to ride bikes until they wore out. In a disciplined atmosphere like that, Post was never likely to hide his feelings with riders.

"If he's not going well; well, you've got to say so," he said. "Most riders don't want to know the truth, but I'm hard on myself as well. You mustn't look for the easy way out."

"So you see riders as what — friends? Employees?"

"Not as friends. Employees. They're not my friends. But I try to have a good relationship with them. And you can relate to some riders more than others. They're all different."

We sipped coffee for a while, brought by his wife, whom he calls *schat*, or Treasure. He wore jacket and jeans. We sat on a big leather sofa with large impressions on the wall of motocross and American football and a life-size painting of a Raleigh rider, arms aloft. It was a tasteful, modern room, large for Holland, where land is scarce and expensive, with a white desk and two telephones on one side and a pile of Panasonic jerseys and a television on the other. If you want an entertaining few moments, steer Post towards the cost of modern riders.

"Ja-a-a! Salaries now are very high. Very high. It costs at least five or six times more than six years ago. For some riders it's ten times as much. But they ask for it and people pay it."

For Jan Janssen, who lives in the same village as Kuiper, those salaries helped make the sport soft.

"We had to be good all the time, from the first of February until the end of October," he said. "It was my duty to make the most of the sponsor's name, to get publicity. There were other good riders on the team, but it was 80 percent on my shoulders to get that publicity. And if you had an off-day, well, you were letting your sponsors down." It reminded me of a parody in *Cycle Sport* in which "Old Pro" writes columns that always concluded "Well, in my day it wasn't like that at all." The difference is that Janssen is a former Tour winner and world champion, and he's still involved with the Zuid-West Hoek club in Bergen-op-Zoom. His views deserve respect.

How much do they get? Hard to say. It's not the kind of thing riders talk about. But during the 1999 Tour there was a fuss when a French rider called Christophe Bassons packed his bags because, he said, he could no longer stand the rejection the bunch showed him after his newspaper columns that came close to suggesting that only he was riding without drugs. Jean-Marie Leblanc, the organizer, suspected Bassons' walkout was *le marketing*, that his price in the post-Tour criteriums would soar without his having to complete the race.

How much would it go up? A day later, the veteran Frenchman Thierry Bourguignon said Bassons could now expect 12,000 francs a ride whereas he, with 10 years' experience, could expect only 7,000 (although he confessed that his wife thought he was worth rather more). Lance Armstrong, he said, was worth 15,000, although at that stage he hadn't yet got his yellow jersey all the way to Paris. There was talk of Armstrong getting a $1 million bonus from his sponsors, but that could be the advantage of riding for a team accustomed to American rather than European expectations in sports.

The figures you see of how much riders get from their teams are suspect. Employers rarely give their employees' wages, first because of privacy but also because they don't want to push the price up for anybody else they may wish to recruit. On the other hand, figures from agents are suspect for the opposite reason, since no agent is likely to suggest a figure lower than reality, and it's in his and his rider's interest to claim something even higher.

The money attributed to individual riders is sometimes out of balance with the known budget of the entire team, or at the very least it's a combination of team retainer and prizes, appearance money, and endorsement fees. At the end of the millennium, for instance, the highest budget quoted for a team in the Tour was 42 million French francs for ONCE, supported by a Spanish lottery and a German bank; the lowest was 15 million for Lotto, a Belgian lottery, and a phone company. Since these are millions of francs and not dollars or pounds, and they have to pay for the whole team, its equipment, and expenses, it becomes clear that salary claims are sometimes over-enthusiastic.

The money is, though, far better than it was, as Post says. The climber Julio Jimenez relates that many Spanish professionals of the sixties earned only 4,000 pesetas a month, or about $30, and worked in the winter as truck drivers or plasterers. The whole Flandria team in Belgium cost just $500,000 a year in the mid-1970s, and that for a team that included Freddy Maertens, Roger De Vlaeminck, and Michel Pollentier — classics and stage winners all. Riders were paid only 10 months a year. Again, Brian Robinson — the first English-speaker to win a Tour stage — was given only his jersey, and a bike, and a few coins of pocket money in the Tour of Switzerland when he came ninth for Cila.

Riding for no more than a jersey and a success bonus was known as competing *à la musette*, after the cloth shoulder bag that was about all a "professional" could expect. When the UCI allowed a category even more tawdry, the so-called independents who were neither amateur nor professional but could wear advertising, and win whatever cash they could, the situation became so ludicrous that Belgium at one time had as many *onafhankelijken* (independents) and professionals as it did amateurs. That's an odd observation in an era when there are neither amateurs nor professionals, but the intention had always been that professionals would be the cream, and the status of independent a stepping stone from one to the other or back to amateur. Instead, for many it became an end in itself. Britain, for instance, had no domestic professionals, but entire fields of independents who considered themselves at the peak of their trade.

That could have been the way it stayed had the UCI not despaired of independents being ultra-cheap professionals that weakened rather than strengthened the sport, and if the French government hadn't belatedly recognized cycle racing as a genuine job and brought it into the scope of the country's minimum wage. Riding *à la musette* was over but "minimum" wage still meant "minimal."

It took a big name to change the system, and it came with Eddy Merckx. Now there was a genuine star capable of demanding a star's wages, albeit less than in other sports, and after Merckx had broken into the select stratosphere of salary and appearance money, Greg LeMond rationalized team contracts into the style we recognize today. Until then they had been what many called feudal.

Whether LeMond pushed retainers as far as credited isn't certain. But certainly they went up, and riders could now — as did LeMond — pick their seasons, instead of riding everything their director underlined in the calendar. As Britain's Barry Hoban said, sometimes it wasn't wise to go well all the time, or a manager would ride you until you were dead.

Janssen again:

> I think the motivation has changed. You get riders saying after the Tour that they're stopping at home because they can't be bothered with criteriums, and that's not attractive to the public. I don't think you're serving the sport doing that, because the more popular cycling is, the better it is for every one of the riders. It's good that they're well paid now, of course, but they have to give everything they've got, and now there are a load of riders who say, "I only want to ride the classics in the spring, and no Tour de France, no Giro, and no Tour of Spain, because it's too hot there, and there are too many mountains, and there's this, and there's that," and there are riders who say they're not going to ride Paris–Roubaix over the bad roads, and no Tour of Flanders in the snow and rain. They pick, and choose their races.

Well, it didn't used to be that way. You got a list of races from your team manager, and you had to ride them. The whole sport has changed. They're not hungry any more. There is so much money to earn now, even for a third-rate rider. Twenty-five years ago, a third-class rider didn't get jam on his bread. So if they got 50 guilders for a criterium, they rode. But now, every rider is well paid, but they don't do much for it. They say "Oh, I've got a good contract from the firm; I'm OK." The hunger to ride well, to succeed, and only then to earn money, is over.

Robert Millar says the Tour is rotten to ride but a good career move. In other words, it can perk up your contract and appearance money. These days a team leader will give his winnings to his team-mates, to reward them but also, of course, to keep them in order. It happened first after a meeting in France in 1953. Present, among others likely to ride for France that year, was Louison Bobet, a tall, handsome man, the first to win three Tours in as many years.

He was a superb athlete but lack of confidence led him to behave like David Niven, the suave, smooth-talking film hero of the era. He longed to move in polite society, and went to absurd lengths to avoid the distasteful. Once, at a dinner-party, a society lady heard he had been in hospital, and asked him to explain. Bobet blushed.

"Ours is a difficult métier," he began awkwardly. "You understand, madame, that we ride many kilometers a year. It gives us certain difficulties."

The woman looked puzzled, and the other riders looked on with cruel interest.

"With our…, with our..." Bobet blushed more deeply. "With our, er, pockets."

"With your pockets, Monsieur Bobet?" the woman asked, now mystified.

Bobet opened his mouth again, and then, as he struggled for polite words, Raphaël Géminiani jumped in, and said, "Oh for heaven's sake, Zonzon, tell her you've got bloody balls."

In 1953 the friction in the French team was so great that halfway through the race Géminiani is said to have emptied a bowl of soup on Bobet's head and stuffed spaghetti in his ears. It's undoubtedly grown with the telling, but it gives you an idea. So how did the two men ever get on the same team? Well, they and the others were brought together by Marcel Bidot, the national selector. He went around the table and asked each how he'd do.

"Can you win?"

"I don't think so, but I can get in the top five," and so on.

When he reached Bobet, the Brittany beau answered: "Yes, I can win if the rest of the team will block for me." When the others stared at him, he added: "And if I win, I'll give all my prizes to my teammates," and that's how the tradition started. A leader needed not only talent but a wallet to secure control. In return he'd get appearance contracts after Paris, and a better deal from his sponsor. But does it still happen? Does the Tour winner give away his prizes in exchange for the few remaining criteriums? Well, not for the criteriums, certainly, but Stephen Roche says he never kept a penny of what he won as team leader. Not just Tour prizes but all his prizes.

"I was one of the lucky ones," he told me in Dublin as he prepared to move to the Côte d'Azur in France ("You'd be surprised how expensive Ireland has become."). "I was on a good whack, and because of that I was paying a lot of tax. If I won £10,000, I'd have to give half of it to the tax man, so I'd only have £5,000 left. Compared to the wages, the prizes are just an extra, especially after tax, so it meant less to me than the other guys. So I used to give 10 percent to the team staff, and the rest to the team for getting me there. That wasn't so common when I started but now it's getting so that it's expected."

Post wasn't much of a stage-race rider, but he was king of the six-days and a name in criteriums and classics. After that he took to running the six-days in Rotterdam and London and working as a team manager. I asked whether the sport had made him rich.

"I don't know what you think of as rich," he countered. "I'm rich in health, that I can do anything, that I can work every day. But *ja*, if you've been working for the best part of 30 years, seven days a week, it stands to reason that you'll earn something."

He retired a few years later, and I assume he's living on the remains of that "something." There was an exercise bike in the room, and he told me that he had no interest in riding a bike on the roads anymore. Since then I've heard that he does. But not half as hard as he used to, I bet.

The End of the Beginning

I N THE TOUR de France, only journalists drive their own cars. The teams, their officials and the race directors collect a range of vehicles provided by a sponsor. The suppliers change over the years but the ones that stood on a garage forecourt on Tuesday July 7, 1998 were Fiats registered with outer-Paris numbers. Willy Voet, a Belgian worker with one of the Tour's most prominent teams, collected his that morning and drove it out through the traffic of Evry, near Paris. His plan was to drive to the start of the Tour de France in Ireland and join riders and other officials on the Festina team, an expensive squad of mainly French riders that included the baby-faced climber Richard Virenque. Like the others, the housewives' favorite for his *mignon* looks was paid by a Spanish watch company through a sports bureau registered in Andorra.

Andorra is outside the tax régime of the European Union and therefore attractive to companies that use its banks. Bruno Roussel, Festina's sports manager in 1998, said Voet was due to take the highway north from Paris to the port of Calais, cross the English Channel by ship to Dover, and then cross Britain to a second ferry to Dun Laoghaire. He would then drive into Dublin itself for the start of the Tour. All should have gone well. There have been only nominal border and customs controls in continental Europe since government ministers signed away travel restrictions as part of European union. Britain and Ireland were outside the agreement but had agreed to a straight-through channel for Customs. Voet was expecting no problems.

Instead of going straight to Calais, he went on a loop that took him back into his native Belgium and then back into France on a minor road between Dronkaert in Belgium and the French village of Neuville-en-Ferrain, near Lille. He reached the border at 6:30 a.m. on July 8 and expected to cross over without slowing. His Fiat, though, stood out. Fiat wanted to catch TV cameras with its advertising logos and more had been added for Festina. The frontier guards waved him into the roadside and asked Voet to step out. One opened the back. And there, in cardboard boxes, was a stash of hypodermic syringes, hundreds of vials of obscure drugs, and treatments for hepatitis-B, an illness associated with needles and injections. The drugs included anabolic steroids and a blood-strengthening agent known as EPO. Within days, the Tour de France had become the Tour de Farce and an already suspicious public learned that Festina systematically provided drugs for its riders and had a slush fund to buy them.

The rest is too well known to tell. Indeed, its legal consequences were still rumbling after Lance Armstrong had ridden down the Champs Elysées with an outsized Stars and Stripes a year later. Some of the riders most shamed in the scandal — including Alex Zülle, who

Willy Voet spent his time in jail after the 1998 drugs scandal thinking about blowing the whistle on drug-taking. His **Massacre à la Chaîne**, translated into Dutch as Injecting and Swallowing, became a huge seller. Plans to publish it in Britain were scuppered by libel laws — Voet keeps back no secrets with the names of those he accuses and whose drug doses he allegedly details. His book damned, above all, French climber Richard Virenque, who claimed he knew nothing of drug-taking.

came second, and Virenque, whom the organizers had told to stay away but was reinstated after the UCI turned wobbly in response to lawyers' letters — rode the 1999 race nevertheless; Voet stood by the road to watch the race pass while wondering whether the next stage of the inquiry would send him back to jail. Before the race had finished, he and Virenque had locked horns in a publishing war, Virenque's *Ma Verité* more or less denying the lists of drugs allegedly supplied to him and reproduced in Voet's *Massacre à la Chaine* (Chain Massacre).

The number of journalists accredited in 1999 rose from 3,500 to 7,500 as newspapers prepared for a still bigger scandal. Thierry Bourguignon said the first stages "felt like being in a funeral cortège" and that the field felt too isolated and lacked the unity to refuse to ride a dangerous causeway that caused a mass crash that critically affected the result. France, the Tour, and cycling held its breath. The yellow jersey sponsor, Crédit Lyonnais, said it wanted out after the UCI forced Virenque back into the sport; Jean-Marie Leblanc, whom Bernard Hinault had found close to tears as the 1998 race crashed round his ears, had his fingers firmly crossed when he called 1999 "The Tour of Redemption."

The feeling of a spring tightening increased rather then lessened as the police stayed away instead of raiding hotels and taking riders away for questioning, as happened in 1998. Rather than smiling that "it hasn't happened," the pessimism among many favored the belief that "It must be tomorrow, then..." In fact it never happened. Leblanc asked for discretion from the national police force and in particular *les stups* — the drugs police — and it stayed away, although whether as a result of Leblanc's intervention was naturally never clear.

It was inevitable that any hint of skullduggery would blossom. A Belgian went home, not for failing a test but because he'd been treated with a potentially test-failing drug. And when it emerged that Armstrong had had a steroid reading early in the race, although not high enough to justify disqualification, it caused a rumpus. Armstrong appeared on Vélo-club with the British ex-pro and TV commentator Paul Sherwen as translator and explained he had used a skin cream for an injury. Sherwen's translation went further and explained it had been for a saddle sore and suggested there were people "perhaps against me [i.e. Armstrong]." Armstrong never said whom and of course he'd never made the claim in the first place, at least on Vélo-club, but relations were thereafter difficult between him and *Le Monde*, the serious daily that had broken the news.

Armstrong was a welcome winner for the Tour. He wasn't French but France's best rider was Virenque, and the nightmare for Leblanc was that the man who'd sought him out for a formal handshake but was still clearly unwelcome would end up winning. Virenque's supporters were fewer on the road but more vocal at each stage finish. His normal smile was subdued "after the difficulties I have experienced this year," and his face cracked properly only when he received the climbers' award in Paris. By then a story had broken that he was asking criterium organizers to choose between him and a list of his critics, of whom there were many.

For France it was a bad Tour, the first time for decades a Frenchman hadn't won a stage. Well, that was *tant pis*, too bad, but at least Armstrong was a fairy-tale winner after testicular cancer. He had conveniently taken off like a rocket 30 years after another Armstrong had stood on the moon (L'Équipe and other papers rejoiced in headlines like ARMSTRONG UNHOOKS THE MOON and ON ANOTHER PLANET), and better still he spoke a little French, took chances, and had a personality. After Miguel Indurain, that was a blessing.

Indurain, to the French, was a mechanic rather than an engineer. He rode as strategically as Anquetil but without the magic. Above all, he lacked personality. Like Anquetil, he dominated time-trials and refused to be shifted in the mountains. But those who stood by the roadside to marvel were disappointed when they tried to go further and like him. A man who could win five Tours in a row, which defeated every attempt since before World War I, should have been the subject of tea-towels, key rings, and even pictures of his bare backside, as Merckx had been in Belgium. Well, in Spain, perhaps he was. But not in France, not in Belgium, nor anywhere else that I happened to be at the time. He was Big Mig, an enigma behind dark glasses, a general who rarely went into open skirmish.

The French, of course, have lost their race, not because an American won in the last of the millennium but because the focus of talent has shifted. Some said it was because France, unlike other nations, had introduced season-long dope tests in the aftermath of the Festina rumpus. Two-speed cycling, they claimed, with France locked to the smaller chainring. But talent flits between nations like a capricious fairy. Once it was the French, then the Belgians, the Italians, then the

French again, and finally the Dutch, the Americans, and the Spanish. Even a Dane has won and Denmark is the bit you have trouble finding on a map.

In each of those countries, cycling becomes big — or at least bigger — in its glory. Danish journalists, who never normally looked further than Scandinavia, came tumbling into France when Bjarne Riis looked like winning. It happened with American journalists for Lance Armstrong, as it had for Greg LeMond. Ed Pavelka, the former editor of *Velo-News* and *Bicycling*, told me before the 1999 Tour: "Every July, *Bicycling*'s news-stand sales skyrocketed as Greg rode around France. The Tour had been covered previously by network TV, so the average non-cyclist knew a little about it. But with Greg at the front, TV pulled all stops. Every weekend we saw extended coverage that was good enough to win Emmy awards. Meanwhile, Sam Abt was writing daily stage reports for the *New York Times,* and *USA Today* was also giving Greg and the race ample ink.

"Things have slid a lot since his retirement, but if Lance stays healthy there could be a revival of mainstream interest. Americans need a homegrown hero to follow among all the Marios, Marcos and Jean-Maries or they won't give a damn. Lance is somewhat known be-

It soon became clear that Festina riders were contributing to a slush fund from which their drugs were supplied. Festina as a team was thrown out of the Tour and Virenque was personally banned in 1999 until lawyers forced his return. Did any of this hurt the sponsor? Hardly. The Spanish watch company said the publicity had sold more watches than ever before and it was back in 1999 as a sponsor.

cause of the attention that non-cycling publications have given to his cancer and comeback." Now, of course, Armstrong is more than "somewhat known" in the USA. And in Europe his name is as familiar on the streets as Mark McGwire is in St Louis or Sammy Sosa in Chicago.

The days have gone when riders were built into gods by newspapers read by people who had rarely seen them. Still more distant is the sepia world of riders chipping their spines with broken wheels or hammering bikes back into shape in country forges. But the show remains a show, just different. It's vast, it's tawdry, and it's heroic. It conjures extremes and demands that men overcome them, and in overcoming them they merely increase the extremes they have to face next time. It lasts longer than any other game in the world, it encompasses death and misery and triumph and exhilaration. It produces melody and discord, it smothers itself in gross commercialism, and yet it remains the biggest free show on earth. It remains the Tour de France and if it didn't exist, nobody today would ever invent it.

We owe a lot to Géo Lefèvre.

23
A Day at the Races

IT HAS TO BE SAID, the Tour is free and therefore it doesn't take place in stadiums. You buy no ticket and you get no guarantee. You may see no more than a glimpse. But what a gloomy way of looking at it. What a miserable way of dismissing the biggest free party on earth.

The start is where you'll see all the riders. The *Brigade Orange*, the heavies in vivid overalls, will set up the Tour village long before you get there. A lot has happened on the Tour before the sun yawns above the horizon. They work through the night in squads that rarely see each other, some building the start, others the finish, and still more who erect crowd barriers at pinch points. They sleep through the day. The work is astonishing. It goes as far as measuring the temperature of the road and dowsing it with water if it's hot enough to melt. They mend broken stretches, a tradition that goes back to when the Tour paid for road repairs to get through the Pyrénées.

Years ago, you could get close to riders. There was less pressure and they were less cosseted and precious. Now they stay behind the barriers patrolled by policemen and arrive an hour before the start to climb to the signing-on house to register. This is where you see Daniel Mangeas earn his pay; he can never know when and in which order the riders will arrive and yet their record will be announced at length to make each a hero.

The work of starting the Tour happens now in the *Village*. Like most of the best places, access is only by pass. The Tour welcomes countless visitors each day and if you fancy your chances you can write at the start of the year or, as a journalist, call at the press trailer and plead your case. At the least you will need a letter of accreditation from a newspaper or magazine or broadcaster and a union or business card that identifies you as a writer, or broadcaster.

The color of the card identifies your status, and within each color there are subtle variations. An *invité de l'étape* for instance, a guest of the stage (one-day accreditation) may let you into the temporary grandstands — a good way of getting one of those round Tour de France cushions — and the press room and soigneurs' area, but it won't get you into the finish line.

Le Village is exclusive. Riders call for a drink after they've signed on, read papers or talk to journalists. It's where reporters collect bags of papers from Crédit Lyonnais, each identified with the journalist's number. That makes *le village* a good place to get close to. You can be sure that every rider will call or get very close.

You may also get to see some sort of show, perhaps from the Coca-Cola cheerleaders — chosen, as at least one unkind journalist has pointed out, for their talent rather than their looks. Reporters are rarely the most couth of people, especially after several weeks' prox-

The Tour de France is not only the world's biggest sports competition but the biggest free attraction. Nobody knows for certain how many see it by the roadside but the atmosphere is that of a giant party. If you don't bring your own home-made posters to display — for a favorite rider or simply "Good luck to everyone" — you won't go home empty-handed. You may get big green fingers to wag, yellow hats to wear, or unappetising food to swallow.

imity to riders and photographers, and the girls take a lot of ribaldry for overflowing their red outfits and putting the stands in danger.

The advertising caravan gathers in front of the race or in the lot set out in the plans distributed before each race, and again in enlarged form before each start. At this stage the drivers are subdued after hard days of getting their right arms sunburned from crawling round France for three weeks. But paid-for enthusiasm starts the moment they're on the road an hour before the riders. With them go the journalists and officials who line up en avant, ahead of the field, to reach the finish before the riders. They follow a route signposted hours before or take shortcuts suggested in the race bible.

The *securité* of the road — a word that means safety rather than security — is *assuré* by 13,000 policeman and 3,500 security guards. Police patrol even tiny junctions from 6 a.m. and stand before obstructions with triangular yellow flags waving above their head to show the way.

The entourage is a kilometer long and starts slowly. The first minutes from the *départ fictif* will be neutralized. The official start, the *départ réel*, happens beneath a *panneau*, or banner, after the main obstacles of the town have passed. Loudspeakers at *Le Village* an-

nounce that race headquarters will close in five minutes. Heavies break it down and carry it off to the next start.

The best way to find the race is through *L'Équipe* or one of the many magazines, of which *L'Équipe*'s sister magazine *Vélo* is the best. *Vélo* gives the whole route along with distances of intermediate towns (often with the number of the road) and descriptions of the arrangements — *Caravane publicitaire: parking de la gare. Départ: 12 heures. Rassemblement du marché. Signature: de 12h 30 à 13h 30. Appel 13h 35. Départ fictif: 13h 40 par la Grande-Rue, boulevard Ernest-Girault, rue de la Libération. Départ réel: 13h 43 sur D.152, route d'Arpajon, à hauteur du panneau entrée Ollainville, soit à 1.24 km du lieu de rassemblement.* You don't need a lot of French, just a bit of sense and imagination. *Vélo* will also tell you the address and number of the tourist office and the nearest camp site.

The rough route is named at a conference in Paris at which riders, old-timers, and anybody else with something to say are interviewed at length in the hope of some insight. Normally the issues are how many mountains there are, which order they come in and over how many days, whether the Alps precede the Pyrénées, and when and where the time trials are. The exact route, down to the individual villages, comes only after discussions with local councils and police forces. Then large yellow signs go up weeks before the race to warn that the road will close for the morning, the afternoon, or the day.

The Tour could once make the race as long as it liked and for decades it really was a circuit of the country. Simpson's death in 1967 brought the intervention of the UCI, though, and organizers across the world faced limits on the length of their races, the individual stages, and the number of rest days. There were limits, too, on the number of new stage races the world could have. It's rare now for any two stages to join up, so you will probably have a journey from one finish to the next day's start.

Watching from the roadside is a gamble. You never know what you'll see. It could be a peloton stretched to a line, a break minutes ahead of the rest, or an amble by a bunch content to recover or prepare. The Tour's *heures de passage* take account of that, publishing schedules for 42 km/h and 38 km/h, or slower in the mountains. The times are adjusted on each side of climbs, slower up one side than down the other.

The yellow and the polkadot jerseys stand out more than the green in a fast bunch. Less obvious is the red and white one worn by the most combative rider. The hierarchy of the cars is red first — number one is Jean-Marie Leblanc's — and blue afterwards. Then come the commissaires with their orange motorcycle helmets, the television and radio commentators, the team cars (on the right, so that the driver can lean out and talk to the riders) and finally the journalists, who travel on the left.

The bonanza is linked by Radio Tour, a multi-lingual service that calls up team cars when riders raise their arms — *"US Postal est demandé"* — and give simple running commentaries. At the word *chute*, the whole row of team cars prepares to repair the devastation of a crash, the cars' order decided by the team's riders in the overall results.

The yellow cars and motorbikes are the neutral service teams, provided for years by the Mavic accessories company. They work in rotation around the bunch, going ahead and waiting for a break. Commissaires with signaling sticks like large, round lollipops keep team cars out of the gap between bunch and break if there's any danger of their forming a bridge or a handicap for riders closing the gap. That's where, if necessary, a neutral car will go. Or, when the field is split, as in the mountains, the neutrals will take a group apiece.

Thierry Babereau will deliver your mail from his Dynapost van. "If you want to write to anybody on the race," he says, "write the name and the stage town and then Dynapost and France." Give it a couple of days and Babereau will find the hotel and take the mail.

The one remaining motorcyclist is the blackboard man, who with his driver spends all month timing the break, and the chasers, writing the significant riders' numbers on his board, adding the *écart*, or gap, and riding up and down to give everybody the news. The job remains essential even when team cars have television sets to watch the coverage up front and some riders have radio earpieces for instructions.

The route is dotted by prime points but they rarely add much attraction, the bunch being unbothered by the money and only the green jersey contenders interested in the bonus points. Far better are the mountains — but you need to get there early. The most popular is Alpe d'Huez, where spectators spend up to two days securing their place. So many crowd the Alpe that it can take until midnight to get back down. After that come the Alpine and Pyrénéean climbs, like the Galibier and the Tourmalet. Beware the Galibier, though, and also the Soulor and Aubisque that can follow the Tourmalet: all are superb but prone to bad weather because of the air currents that surround them. The Aubisque is also narrow and winding. Of the four, the Tourmalet is best because it gives spectacular views down the way the riders are coming. There's also a bar at the top and at the ski station halfway up.

The roads close three hours or more before the riders get there, although the police will often let you through on a bike if the riders aren't too close behind. Many climbs have cyclists' signs giving the gradient ahead and the distance to the summit. Do, though, stick to the edge of the road. Maniacs run out every year, distracting and handicapping the riders. The competitors get frustrated and occasionally hit out. And sometimes they've been fetched off.

You can watch the Tour move towards you thanks to spectators with televisions — although expect a crowd. But take a radio and listen to France-Info (the rolling news channel up around 105 FM) or France-Info down at the other end of the dial. Europe 1 is also good.

The finish is a gamble. Early in the race and at traditional places like Bordeaux, there'll be a sprint. You won't see much because of the crowds and the speed but you'll see the race unfold by watching the huge TV screen — *l'écran géant*. It'll be set short of the finish so that those who can't see the line get a better view of the race instead. Three hours before the finish the last structures of the finish go up and red-overalled men from ESP Publicité paint the advertising slogans on the road. I tried to engage one in conversation once as he kneeled with a colleague and laid out the stencils to spray FIAT in blue and white five times by the finish line.

"More than a hundred during the race, m'sieur," he said and that's all I could get out of him before he climbed back into his red van decorated with an ESP rider with hands aloft. I sneaked a look inside and saw, not wholly to my surprise, huge tubs of paint.

The arch that carries the *flambe rouge* for the last kilometer goes up at the same time as the podium, a big, grey shell-like structure that inflates from a truck with the help of an air pump. Down at the Dynapost van, Thierry Babereau prepares his racks of mail for the riders, caravan, and journalists. He won't get to deliver them until everybody's got back to the hotels, and then his real work starts.

"If you want to write to anybody on the race," he says as his colleagues chat and sip coffee around a table at the van's entrance, "all you have to do is write the name and then the stage town and then Dynapost and France." Give it a couple of days and the mail and Babereau and the others will find their hotels and take in the mail.

There are metal racks on the inside wall of the van, each with the name of a team.

"We keep records of who gets how much," Babereau said. "Would you like one?" I said I would, and he tapped a computer and pulled out a table of who had received what by Bordeaux. "Lance Armstrong had the most for a while," he said. "A lot from America, but also from England and other countries." The number against his name showed 187. "But suddenly all the post is for Thierry Bourguignon, because he's been on television a lot lately and people like him." He'd been kept busy with 649. That was nothing, though, compared to the 843 for Richard Virenque. Generally, though, mail was down. Bordeaux was two days before the end, so there was little time to make up the numbers. In 1995, Virenque had 1,825, Miguel Indurain 1,674, Claudio Chiapucci 245, and Jacky Durand (*lanterne rouge* in 1999) 188.

Across the road is the *zone technique*, where TV and radio crews gather. Their trucks stand in long corridors with cables lying unprotected between them. Engineering types in T-shirts and unkempt hair show no interest in the racing, although with an hour to go the radio men are already editing tapes ready to broadcast. Spanish TV technicians are more concerned with preparing a salad.

The crowd starts gathering four hours before the riders. By two hours it is heavy, and with an hour to go there's no chance of getting near the line or even the first rows of onlookers. That sounds an imposition, but the point of being at the finish isn't so much to see the race, although that's what everyone says, as to savor the atmosphere, to be part of it, to be there.

The first team trucks and buses come through with an hour to go, cheered by partisan sections of the crowd, and then a growing stream of journalists, photographers, and others, many of whom time their arrival to get a free lunch in the *salle de presse*, a town hall or conference center where they sit at long tables as if they were eating school dinners, tap their computers and watch rows of television sets. In a room behind them, photographers unload digital pictures into their computers, crop and label them, and E-mail them to their newsrooms. Outside, the Tour's souvenir shops have opened for business, occasional sponsors may be holding stage shows and throwing out hats and T-shirts, and squads of extra police march in semi-formation as their commanders detail their positions.

Immediately beyond the finish are the eight galleries of TV commentary positions, with French TV closest to the line. They look like passengers in double-decker buses, the commentators just visible through the windows as they follow the race on TV screens. Beyond them is the grey, oyster-shell podium with curved, Hollywood-style aluminum steps. To the left and right are blue-cushioned silver barrels on which the day's guests sit to be introduced to the prizewinners by

The col d'Aubisque has been the scene of great battles on its narrow, winding roads, and it was where Wim van Est disappeared over the edge in Holland's first yellow jersey. It is, though, notoriously prone to mist, and the bar at the top is the only shelter.

Bernard Hinault. The advertising screen behind the podium slides up to reveal fresh advertising as each sponsor's jersey is handed over.

Opposite is the second five-deep row of red plastic seats built into a scaffold grandstand for guests of the day. The other is on the line itself. The dope control caravan, prominent to convey a message, is alongside the podium. Its two side windows are shielded by grey plastic. And then beyond that is the open-sided studio for Vélo-club. The whole ends with a catchment area for the advertising caravan, which rolls through for an hour before the finish as women — and they always are women and frequently blond — throw knickknacks into the crowd. No flat surface is without an advertisement. All in all, there is a deep atmosphere of activity without anything actually happening.

And then suddenly the organizers' blue, and finally the red cars, the first phalanx of motorcycle outriders, and then almost as an anticlimax, the sprint of riders for the line. They run into the semicircle of photographers, TV and radio crews, and soigneurs, creating a colorful traffic jam beneath Vélo-club before riding on to find the team cars that have been diverted into the finish or turning back and heading for their hotel.

Vélo will tell you where the riders are staying, although not necessarily the teams. It's not hard to find out, although the benefits of going there are less obvious. Riders arrive by bike or more often in their bus and go indoors with only a handful of satisfied autograph hunters. You can stand outside for as long as you like but the chances that a rider will emerge are slim.

By the time you've gathered your breath, the *Brigade Orange* have begun taking down the barriers and loading them noisily into trucks. The police have reopened the approaches to the finish, although not the *arrivée* itself, and the first escapees from the mêlée have found their way to the bars and restaurants. The Tour's offices in Issy-les-Moulineaux will be almost empty. The staff return after the Champs Elysées... and go off on two weeks' holiday. The day they return, someone will be working out how many barriers, how many Coca-Cola inflatable cushions to protect their corners, how many blue Fiat signs on each side of the finish line.

The Tour has known death and scandal and sheer bad taste. But since 1903 only world wars have managed to halt it.

Appendix 1

100 Things You Didn't Know About the Tour

1: The smallest number of starters was in 1919, when just 11 set off. Of years unaffected by war, there were 60 in 1903 and 1905.

2: The Swiss Urs Zimmerman was disqualified in 1991 for driving from Nantes to Pau because he disliked flying. The bunch went on strike for 40 minutes until he was reinstated.

3: Jean Robic, accused of throwing his bottle at a spectator, said he couldn't have because he'd filled it with lead to get down the Tourmalet faster.

4: Tom Simpson pioneered modern saddles in the Tour by sticking part of his wife's handbag to an early plastic saddle.

5: The highest dropout rate was in 1919, when 84 percent of riders abandoned.

6: A women's race, the Tour Féminin, ran from 1984 to 1989, when it was canceled for lack of sponsorship. It ran the last 35 to 50 miles of some stages, two hours before the Tour.

7: The 11th Tour started on June 28, 1914, the day a Serbian nationalist assassinated Archduke Francis Ferdinand and prompted World War I.

8: French veterans Antonin Magne and André Leducq crossed the line arm-in-arm and ahead of the bunch to end their careers at the Parc des Princes in 1938. They were 34, born 12 days apart, made their Tour debuts in 1927, and each won twice.

9: A toe amputated during the Tour from climber René Vietto is now kept in preserving liquid in a bar in Marseille.

10: Jacques Goddet's favorite was Frenchman Roger Walkowiak, the least popular with the public. He won an easy but fast Tour in 1956 without taking a stage and never rode again at the same level. He worked in a factory when he retired after 12 years — not typical for a Tour winner. "But he rode with his head as well as his legs and never missed the right move," says Goddet. He's also Jean-Paul Ollivier's favorite.

11: The Hôtel Catala at Baudéan near the Tourmalet has rooms named after Jacques Anquetil, Eddy Merckx, and others. The hotel also has a picture of Bernard Hinault in his yellow jersey, mounted above the badger that gave him his nickname.

12: Most noticeable figure at the end of every stage was team manager Antonin Magne. Why? Because he always wore a beret and a cowman's white raincoat.

13: Antonin Magne couldn't have worn his yellow jerseys — he lost them all after the German invasion.

14: André Leducq was arrested by the Germans during the war. Suddenly his interrogator looked at him and said, "Go free." Leducq later teased Raymond Poulidor: "You see, Raymond? It helps to have won the Tour de France."

15: French police marshaling the Tour had to leave their guns at the Channel Tunnel when the Tour came to England and Ireland. The crowd in England cheered each time a British bobby overruled his French counterpart.

16: Television cost Lucien Van Impe victory. He had two minutes at the foot of Alpe d'Huez when a TV car ran into his rear wheel. Bernard Thévenet passed him to win.

17: Georges Speicher — the Frenchman dragged from a night club to win the world championship — brought *L'Auto* its record sale of 845,045 copies when he won the 1933 Tour, the first to cross France counterclockwise.

18: The first foreigner to win a stage was Charles Laeser of Switzerland, at Bordeaux in 1903. But he didn't finish that year's race, nor the next.

19: Three riders have won eight stages in a Tour. Charles Pélissier did it in 1930, Eddy Merckx in 1970 and 1974, and Freddy Maertens in 1976.

20: One of the Tour's most famous photographs shows Gerben Karstens of Holland dying beneath his crushed bicycle. When the photographers had gone, he walked away with a smile.

21: Bic manager Maurice De Muer set up a table under a tree at 50 miles and gave his team a picnic in the 20th stage of 1970. Luis Ocaña, Jan Janssen, and Jean-Marie Leblanc (now the Tour organizer) were fined 50 francs for stopping outside the eating zone.

22: Eddy Merckx's nickname of Cannibal was coined by a little-known French rider, Christian Raymond.

23: Jacques Goddet's real name is Jean-François. He was born in 1905.

24: Jacques Anquetil knew his priorities when he climbed off to end his Tour career on the climb from Chamonix to St. Etienne in 1966. He dropped to the back of the bunch, reached for a comb, and only then answered questions.

25: Switzerland's Hugo Koblet kept a comb, a moistened sponge and a can of cologne in his pocket. Over the line, and sometimes before it, he'd comb his hair, wipe away the sweat, and spray on cologne before meeting fans. Singer Jacques Grello nicknamed him "the pedaller of charm."

26: Just as it seemed Raymond Poulidor might finally win in 1968, a press motorcycle missed a turn and crashed into his back wheel.

27: The last but one in the first Tour de France, Desvages, rode a British BSA freewheel. The others rode fixed wheels.

28: Maurice Garin may have been a cheat but Desgrange said, "I have kept for this Maurice Garin the admiration that I had as a child for the heroes of legend."

29: Tour passes come in yellow (all areas), blue (ahead of the race and stage organizers), green (press), pink (caravan), grey (salesmen).

30: Svend Novrup, Denmark's cycling commentator for Eurosport, is a world authority on bridge.

31. The first cinema film based on the Tour was *Le Roi de la Pédale* in 1925. It starred an actor called Biscot.

32. In 1935 the prize list passed a million (old) francs, but legend says the first prize was never publicized so that the winner could make his own deal with the tax office.

33. In 1960 the bunch stopped at Colombey-les-Deux-Églises to greet General de Gaulle at the foot of his garden. Pierre Beuffeuil caught the bunch after chasing back from a flat, went straight past and won the stage.

34. The last Tour to finish at the Parc des Princes was 1967, when Roger Pingeon won. The old pink track in Paris's 16th arrondissement was demolished and the name is now associated with rugby.

35. A film, *23 Days in July*, followed Phil Anderson's progress in 1981 as the first Australian to wear the yellow jersey.

36. There were three times as many Colombian journalists as riders when the country put up a team in 1983.

37. Greg LeMond once referred to the Claudio Chaiapucci as "Claudio Capuccino, or whatever his name is." He apologized next day.

38. The film *Pour le Maillot Jaune* in 1939 starred Jacques Goddet's sister-in-law, Meg Lemonnier.

39. Columbia Pictures' *The Yellow Jersey*, starring Dustin Hoffman, has never been screened.

40. Feel for Arne Jonsson, who came from Denmark, then had to go home before the prologue when he forgot his cycling shoes. He failed to finish in both 1959 and 1960.

41. The Tour in the 1970s banned anything but the name of the team on jerseys. It cost 1,000 francs a man in fines each day when Bic had the logo Briquet Bic (Bic lighters).

42. Antonin Magne believed fan mail brought bad luck. But a letter in 1931 told him Jef Demuysère planned to attack between Charleville and Malo-les-Bans. Demuysère attacked exactly as predicted. Magne was ready. The two won by 17 minutes.

43. Octave Lapize despaired so much at being outnumbered by Belgians on the Portet d'Aspet that he returned to the bottom. He told Desgrange: "How can anyone fight in such conditions?" That evening all his team dropped out as well.

44. Jacques Goddet introduced the green points jersey to counter the domination of Fausto Coppi in the mountains, the stages, and overall. The first wearer was Switzerland's Fritz Schaer.

45: The first leaders from start to end were Ottavio Bottecchia in 1924 and Romain Maes in 1935.

46: Many riders have become team managers, but few with Cyrille Guimard's success. Four years after quitting with knee injuries, Guimard convinced van Impe he could win in 1976, the first of the manager's seven Tour wins.

47: The first canceled stage was to Fontaine-au-Pire in 1982. Striking factory workers obstructed the road. Farmers blocked the start at Orcières with tractors on the 16th stage, but the race eventually started.

48: Denis Roux of Canada said of the women's Tour: "Females, they're a mystery to me. I've decided to change nothing, to apply the same methods as with the men. But I may put things differently. You can tell a guy he's got a fat ass... but not a girl."

50: The record for stage wins is 34 by Eddy Merckx. Bernard Hinault won 28, André Leducq 25, and André Darrigade 22.

51. The first time trial was 90 km between La Roche-sur-Yon and Nantes in 1934.

52. Joop Zoetemelk started a record 16 Tours and finished them all.

53. The first finish on the Champs-Elysées was in 1975, won by the Belgian sprinter Walter Godefroot.

54. A Frenchman punched Eddy Merckx in the stomach on the Puy-de-Dôme in 1975. Merckx carried on to the finish, wheeled down the hill to identify his attacker, then pressed for a nominal franc in damages. His attacker was fined $100.

55. Italian champion Ottavio Bottechia was found dead by a country road two weeks before the 1927 Tour. A farmer claimed on his deathbed that he had thrown a rock at Bottechia and accidentally killed him after seeing him eating his grapes.

56. Peeing on the move is said to have been pioneered by Luxembourg's Charly Gaul. He was so big-headed that the bunch broke unwritten rules and attacked the moment he stopped. Gaul's technique later became widespread.

57. Bic publicist Christian Durras ran inside a church for a better view of Bernard Labourette winning in the Pyrénées. The pastor entered and Durras felt he ought to pray. But he leaped to the window when he saw his rider and shouted, "Bravo! We won!" The priest looked out, smiled and offered Durras a glass of wine.

58. The Tour crossed the Iron Curtain for the first time in 1987 for three days in West Berlin. Lech Piasecki, a Pole who grew up less than 200 km from the Berlin Wall, became first Eastern European to wear yellow. He didn't finish.

59. The first Eastern European team came in 1989, the year the Berlin Wall came down. Russia entered but didn't win a stage until Dimitri Konyshev in 1990.

60. Poland's Zenon Jaskula was the first East European in the top three. At the start of 1993 he was a promising amateur who'd become an unknown professional. But he won at Saint Lary-Soulan in the Pyrénées and moved into third place after the final time trial.

61. Legend says Maurice Garin's father sold him to a chimney sweep for a wheel of cheese.

62. The first transfer between stages was from Lille to Douai in 1906.

63. The same three riders took the same three top positions in 1978 and 1979 — Bernard Hinault, followed by Joop Zoetemelk and Joaquim Agostinho.

64. Henri Desgrange was so upset by riders idling in the 11th stage in 1928 that he stopped the bunch at the Marseille track and ended the day with an elimination race, the last rider each lap dropping out.

65. Nicolas Frantz of Luxembourg said Desgrange told him he wasn't to beat Ottavio Bottechia in 1924 because he didn't have the caliber or image of a Tour winner. His manager told Frantz he'd never race again if he didn't agree.

66. Desgrange, displeased at Maurice De Waele's victory in 1929, announced, "My race has been won by a corpse."

67. Tour winner André Leducq survived two world wars only to die while diving in 1980. He was 76.

68. The Brooklyn team didn't make the 1975 Tour because the sponsor had been kidnaped. There was too little money left for the team by the time the ransom was paid

69. The Tour first set wheel on the Champs Elysées at 3 a.m. on July 13, 1908, where start formalities were conducted under portable gas lights.

70. Henri Pélissier used to sandpaper his wooden rims. "I can save 50 g, and 50 g on a revolving part is worth 2 kg on the frame," he claimed.

71: The Tour uses geo-stationary satellites to give rolling time checks and to show TV viewers the remaining distance to a handful of meters.

72: There are more than 1,200 TV journalists on the Tour and more than 100 trucks to carry the satellite dishes, mobile studios, and other gear.

73: Phil Liggett, the voice of TV cycling in the U.S. and Britain, was once an elephant keeper at Chester, near Liverpool.

74: The Briton John Clarey entertained the race while stubbornly remaining its last rider by having his moustache sprayed each morning with plant feed.

75: Sean Kelly and Eric Vanderaerden were moved from sixth to last in the bunch finish at Rheims in 1986 after a full fight in the middle of the sprint.

76. The Tour's greatest cartoonist was René Pellarin, who used the name Pellos to draw frowning mountains and hammer-bearing winds around brilliant caricatures of riders in the 13 Tours he followed. He would sit in trees, in caves, and in ditches to find the peace he needed to work. He died in 1988.

77. Steven Rooks got home from winning the mountains prize in the 1988 Tour to find that customers had painted red polkadots all over his favorite restaurant in Warmenhuisen, north-west Holland.

78. Bad luck for East Germany's Uwe Ampler. He dropped back to his car for permission to retire with a knee injury. A commissaire hooted, Ampler wobbled, caught his bars on the car and crashed to the road.

79. Britain's Barry Hoban is the only rider to have competed against the first three five-time winners, Anquetil, Merckx and Hinault.

80. Laurent Fignon became so cross with reporters asking why he'd been dropped in 1988 that he threw his *bidon* at them. He was fined 1,000 francs — and later diagnosed as having a tapeworm.

81: Winner Laurent Fignon has his own web site to comment on the Tour. It's at www.laurent-fignon.com

82: Chris Boardman rode a plastic-framed Lotus bike of the sort he'd used to break the world hour record. to set a record prologue speed of 55.15 km/h in Lille in 1993.

83: Most Tour riders speak at least some French — but not as well as pioneering Australian Russell Mockridge, who set himself the target of understanding horse-race commentaries... and succeeded.

84 Every Tour has ended in Paris, except for the first, which ended at Ville-d'Avray, outside the city, before an "honorary finish" at the Parc des Princes.

85: André Darrigade was leading a finish sprint when he hit an official who'd leaned out for a better view. Darrigade was injured and the official killed.

86: Tour organizers fearing another death like Simpson's, arranged the next finish on Mont Ventoux for the end of the day when the air was cooler. But Eddy Merckx still needed oxygen after winning alone.

87: Early Flemish riders were nicknamed *flahutes* for the way they rode uncomplainingly in groups in the Belgian winter winds, like wild ducks.

86: In 1949 the Belgian classics king, Rik van Steenbergen, sprinted half a lap too early on the Bordeaux track... and lost the stage. Eyebrows and suspicions were raised.

87: Green jersey Freddy Maertens first came to notice as a boy of 14 — when he kept asking questions in a bunch of training professionals — while riding a bike laden with newspapers.

88: Barry Hoban described Eddy Merckx as "the biggest cry-baby in the business... if he is beaten it is because of some mishap; if someone else wins then either Eddy would have won if he had been riding or the other man beat nobody."

89: A Dutch woman turned up at Bernard Hinault's house in Brittany and demanded he make love to her immediately. When he refused, she began swearing. Hinault said he recognized they were swear words because he'd heard them from Dutch cyclists.

90: Jacques Anquetil was once asked whether women liked to ride bikes because of the stimulation of their saddle. He thought it over and said there could be something in it because he'd had the same sort of feeling himself now and then.

91: The Tour once rode so fast on a stage to Marseille that the riders had showered and left before the mayor arrived. He never let the race into the city again.

92: The prime minister of Italy once begged Gino Bartali to win a stage, to take the pressure of public attention off him. Bartali won seven of the next 21 stages and set a speed record that stood for six years.

93: The Spanish climber Federico Bahamontes often spoke of himself in the third person — "Federico was feeling tired today, but he will be stronger tomorrow."

94: Antonin Magne was away in the lead for hour after hour on dusty roads in a heatwave. The truck preceding the race kicked up clouds of dust. After long misery, a helper handed up a bottle. Sadly he let go of it too early, it dropped into Magne's front wheel and the Frenchman spread-eagled on to the road.

95: An American journalist in 1966 described a typical backmarker as, "He may have lost his toenails from the constant forward pressure... his backside may be pocked by suppurating ulcers, and his mind so addled by amphetamine that he is not sure of his name, but he is a hero, a major athletic figure, a finisher in the Tour de France."

96: The first rider to use titanium in the Tour was Luis Ocaña, who had an experimental titanium headset in 1971.

97: The first stage to be canceled because of the weather was on July 8, 1996, when midsummer snow closed the Iseran and Galibier passes. Riders rode just the last 46 km, where Bjarne Riis of Denmark won at Sestriere.

98: Alex Virot, the pioneer of radio broadcasting, died with his driver when their motorbike plunged into a ravine on the 16th stage in 1957.

99. Raymond Poulidor advertises insurance policies on French television.

100. Louison Bobet, who with his dapper manners and private plane aspired to be an aristocrat, was born above a bread shop.

Appendix 2

The 20th Century's English-Speakers in the Tour

United States

Norman Ailvis	1990 142nd
Frankie Andreu	1992 110th, 1993 89th, 1994 89th, 1995 82nd, 1995 82nd, 1996 111th, 1997 79th, 1998 58th, 1999 65th
Lance Armstrong	1993 DNF (stage win, Verdun), 1994 DNF, 1995 36th (stage win, Toulouse), 1996 DNF, 1999 1st (maillot jaune, four stage wins: Puy-de-Fou prologue, Metz, Sestriere, Futuroscope TT)
Andy Bishop	1988 135th, 1990 116th, 1991 126th, 1992 DNF
Jonathon Boyer	1981 32nd, 1982 23nd, 1983 12th, 1984 31st, 1987 98th
Jeff Bradley	1987 DNF
Chris Carmichael	1986 DNF
Mike Carter	1991 DNF
Alexis Grewal	1986 DNF
Tyler Hamilton	1997 69th, 1998 51st, 1999 13th
Andy Hampsten	1986 4th, 1987 16th, 1988 15th, 1989 22nd, 1990 11th, 1991 8th, 1992 4th (stage win, l'Alpe d'Huez), 1993 8th
Eric Heiden	1986 DNF
George Hincapie	1996 DNF, 1997 104th, 1998 53rd, 1999 78th
Marty Jamison	1997 96th, 1998 48th
Bobby Julich	1997 17th, 1998 3rd, 1999 DNF
Ron Kiefel	1986 96th, 1987 82nd, 1988 69th, 1989 73rd, 1990 83rd, 1991 138th, 1992 DNF
Roy Knickman	1988 DNF, 1989 DNF
Greg LeMond	1984 3rd, 1985 2nd (stage win, Lac de Vassivière), 1986 1st (maillot jaune, stage win Superbagnères, 1989 1st (maillot jaune, three stage wins: Rennes, Aix-les-Bains, Paris), 1990 1st (maillot jaune), 1991 7th (maillot jaune), 1992 DNF, 1994 DNF
Kevin Livingston	1997 38th, 1998 17th, 1999 36th
Davis Phinney	1986 DNF (stage win, Perret), 1987 DNF (stage win, Bordeaux), 1988 105th, 1990 153rd
Jeff Pierce	1986 80th, 1987 88th (stage win, Paris), 1988 DNF, 1989 86th
Bob Roll	1986 63rd, 1987 DNF, 1990 132nd
Doug Shapiro	1985 74th, 1986 DNF
Jonathan Vaughters	1999 DNF
Chris van de Velde	1999 85th

Great Britain

Bob Addy	1968 DNF
John Andrews	1959 DNF, 1960 DNF
Dave Bedwell	1955 DNF
Chris Boardman	1994 DNF (maillot jaune, stage win Lille prologue), 1995 DNF, 1996 39th, 1997 DNF (maillot jaune, stage win Rouen prologue), 1998 DNF (maillot jaune, stage win Dublin prologue), 1999 119th
Stan Brittain	1958 69th, 1960 DNF, 1961 DNF
Bill Burl	see Canada (mixed team)
Pete Chisman	1967 DNF
John Clarey	1968 63rd
Ron Coe	1958 DNF, 1961 DNF

186

Vin Denson	1961 DNF, 1964 72nd, 1965 87th, 1966 DNF, 1967 DNF, 1968 62nd
Malcolm Elliott	1987 94th, 1988 90th
Derek Green	1968 DNF
Derek Harrison	1968 DNF, 1969 32nd
Peter Hill	1967 DNF
Albert Hitchen	1961 DNF, 1967 DNF
Tony Hoar	1955 69th
Barry Hoban	1964 65th, 1967 62nd (stage win, Sète), 1968 33rd (stage win, Sallanches), 1969 67th (two stage wins, Bordeaux, Brive), 1970 DNF, 1971 41st, 1972 70th, 1973 43rd (two stage wins, Argelès, Versailles), 1974 37th (stage win, Montpellier), 1975 68th (stage win, Bordeaux), 1977 41st, 1978 65th
Charles Holland	1937 DNF
Graham Jones	1980 49th, 1981 20th, 1983 69th, 1984 DNF, 1987 DNF
Stan Jones	1955 DNF
John Kennedy	1960 DNF
Fred Krebs	1955 DNF
Kenneth Laidlaw	1961 65th
Bill Lawrie	see Australia (rode in GB team)
Colin Lewis	1967 84th, 1968 DNF
Bob Maitland	1955 DNF
Arthur Metcalfe	1967 69th, 1968 DNF
Robert Millar	1983 14th (stage win, Luchon), 1984 4th (climbers' jersey, stage win Guzet-Neige), 1985 11th, 1986 DNF, 1987 19th, 1988 DNF, 1989 10th (stage win, Superbagnères), 1990 DNF, 1991 72nd, 1992 18th, 1993 24th
Ken Mitchell	1955 DNF
Ian Moore	1961 DNF
Bill Nickson	1977 DNF
George O'Brien	1961 DNF
Hugh Porter	1968 DNF
Bernard Pusey	1955 DNF
Alan Ramsbottom	1962 45th, 1963 16th
Harry Reynolds	1960 DNF
Brian Robinson	1955 29th, 1956 14th, 1957 DNF, 1958 DNF (stage win, Brest), 1959 19th (stage win, Châlon-sur-Saône), 1960 26th, 1961 53rd
Pete Ryall	1961 DNF
Seamus Ryan	see Ireland (mixed team)
Max Sciandri	1990 154th, 1992 DNF, 1993 71st, 1995 47th (stage win, Saint-Etienne), 1996 DNF, 1997 67th, 1998 DNF
Norman Sheil	1960 DNF
Tom Simpson	1960 29th, 1961 DNF, 1962 6th (maillot jaune), 1964 14th, 1965 DNF, 1966 DNF, 1967 DNF
Ian Steel	1955 DNF
Vic Sutton	1959 37th, 1960 DNF
Adrian Timmis	1987 70th
Paul Watson	1987 DNF
Bev Wood	1955 DNF
Michael Wright	1964 56th, 1965 24th (stage win, Auxerre), 1967 DNF (stage win, Strasbourg), 1968 28th, 1969 71st, 1972 55th, 1973 57th (stage win, Aubagne), 1974 57th
Sean Yates	1984 91st, 1985 122nd, 1986 112th, 1987 DNF, 1988 59th (stage win, Wasquehal), 1989 45th, 1990 119th, 1991 DNF, 1992 83rd, 1993 88th, 1994 71st (maillot jaune), 1995 DNF

Canada

Steve Bauer	1985 10th, 1986 23rd, 1987 74th, 1988 4th (maillot jaune, stage win Machecoul), 1989 15th, 1990 27th (maillot jaune), 1991 97th, 1992 DNF, 1993 101st, 1994 DNF, 1995 101st
Bill Burl	1937 DNF

| Gordon Fraser | 1997 DNF |
| Alex Stieda | 1986 120th (maillot jaune) |

Australia

Don Allan	1974 103rd , 1975 85th
Phil Anderson	1981 10th (maillot jaune), 1982 5th (maillot jaune, stage win Nancy), 1983 9th, 1984 10th, 1985 5th, 1986 39th, 1987 27th, 1989 38th, 1990 71st, 1991 45th (stage win, Quimper), 1992 81st, 1993 84th, 1994 69th
Ernie Baimbridge	1928 DNF
John Beasley	1952 DNF, 1955 DNF
Stephen Hodge	1989 83rd, 1990 34th, 1991 67th, 1992 93rd, 1994 83rd, 1995 64th
Patrick Jonker	1994 DNF, 1996 12th, 1997 62nd, 1998 34th
Don Kirkham	1914 17th
Richard Lamb	1931 35th
Bill Lawrie	1967 DNF
Robbie Mc Ewen	1997 117th, 1998 89th, 1999 122nd (stage win, Paris)
Russell Mockridge	1955 64th
Ivor Munro	1914 20th
Ossie Nicholson	1931 DNF
Stuart O'Grady	1997 109th, 1998 54th (maillot jaune), 1999 4th (sprinters' jersey)
Hubert Opperman	1928 18th, 1931 12th
Percy Osborne	1928 38th
Alan Peiper	1984 95th, 1985 86th, 1987 DNF, 1990 DNF, 1992 26th
Neil Stephens	1992 74th, 1993 DNF, 1994 52nd, 1995 60th, 1996 49th, 1997 54th (stage win, Colmar)
Scott Sunderland	1996 101st
Shane Sutton	1987 DNF
Jay Sweet	1999 DNF
Frank Thomas	1931 DNF
Henk Vogels	1997 99th 121st
Michael Wilson	1988 50th, 1989 69th

Ireland

Martin Earley	1985 60th, 1986 46th, 1987 65th, 1988 DNF, 1989 44th (stage win, Pau), 1990 DNF, 1991 DNF, 1992 80th
Shay Elliott	1956 DNF, 1958 48th, 1959 DNF, 1961 47th, 1963 61st (maillot jaune, stage win Roubaix), 1964 DNF
Sean Kelly	1978 34th (stage win, Poitiers), 1979 38th, 1980 29th (two stage wins, Saint-Etienne, Fontenay-sous-Bois), 198 48th (stage win, Thonon), 1982 15th (sprinters' jersey, stage win Pau), 1983 7th (maillot jaune, sprinters' jersey), 1984 5th, 1985 4th (sprinters' jersey), 1987 DNF, 1988 46th, 1989 9th (sprinters' jersey), 1990 30th, 1991 DNF, 1992 43rd
Paul Kimmage	1986 131st, 1987 DNF, 1989 DNF
Laurence Roche	1991 153rd
Stephen Roche	1983 13rd, 1984 25th, 1985 3rd (stage win, Pau), 1986 48th, 1987 1st (maillot jaune, stage win Futuroscope) 1989 DNF, 1990 44th, 1991 DNF, 1992 9th (stage win, La Bourboule), 1993 13th
Seamus Ryan	1961 DNF

New Zealand

Nathan Dahlberg	1988 144th, 1989 DNF
Paul Jezzon	1979 DNF
Eric McKenzie	1982 87th, 1983 DNF, 1985 127th, 1986 DNF
Stephen Swart	1987 DNF, 1994 112th, 1995 109th
Harry Watson	1928 28th

Index